I0188446

# THE LIBERATION OF BULGARIA

## War Notes in 1877

### BY WENTWORTH HUYSHE

*Late War Correspondent of the "Times" (Soudan, 1885),
and "New York Herald" (Bulgaria, 1877).*

**The Naval & Military Press Ltd**

published in association with

**FIREPOWER**
**The Royal Artillery Museum**
Woolwich

Published by
**The Naval & Military Press Ltd**
Unit 10 Ridgewood Industrial Park,
Uckfield, East Sussex,
TN22 5QE England
Tel: +44 (0) 1825 749494
Fax: +44 (0) 1825 765701
www.naval–military-press.com

*in association with*

**FIREPOWER**
**The Royal Artillery Museum, Woolwich**
www.firepower.org.uk

The Naval & Military
Press

MILITARY HISTORY AT YOUR
FINGERTIPS

… a unique and expanding series of reference works

Working in collaboration with the foremost
regiments and institutions, as well as acknowledged
experts in their field, N&MP have assembled a
formidable array of titles including technologically
advanced CD-ROMs and facsimile reprints of
impossible-to-find rarities.

*In reprinting in facsimile from the original, any imperfections are inevitably reproduced
and the quality may fall short of modern type and cartographic standards.*

*The*
*Liberation*
*of*
*Bulgaria*

THE DEATH GRIP.

THE

# LIBERATION

OF

# BULGARIA

## War Notes in 1877

*By*

### *WENTWORTH HUYSHE*

*Late War Correspondent of the "Times" (Soudan, 1885), and
"New York Herald" (Bulgaria, 1877).*

"QUIS FUROR EST ATRAM BELLIS ARCESSERE MORTEM!
IMMINET, ET TACITO CLAM VENIT ILLA PEDE."

WITH ILLUSTRATIONS AND MAPS

*LONDON*

BLISS, SANDS AND FOSTER

CRAVEN STREET, STRAND, W.C.

1894

# PREFACE

IT is rather late in the day to publish notes which were taken on the battle-fields of 1877, during the memorable struggle for the freedom of Bulgaria. Until now I have not found leisure in an extremely active life to get them into book form, but I have clung to the hope that they may be found worth resuscitating.

It was my fortune to represent a great transatlantic journal during the war of 1877, and since then I have known the storm and stress of another campaign. Many of the incidents of the Bulgarian War of Liberation, and my impressions of them, interesting at the time, have vanished into the limbo of forgotten things. But certain events, tragic, comic, serio-comic — for the great Drama of War has varied scenes — stand out from the dim background in the full glare of memory. Their terror, their sadness, their laughter, remain.

Young Bulgaria is so constantly *en évidence* before Europe that I hope these notes, made at the time when her then great ally was struggling that she should be free, may not be wholly uninteresting.

W. H.

# CONTENTS

# CHAPTER I.

## How J got my Pass to the Front.

IT is April of 1877. War has been declared
by Russia; the Muscovite battalions, massed
for months along the Pruth, are in motion; the
White Czar has bid his children advance in
God's name; he himself has arrived at Kisheneff
with all the pomp, pride, and circumstance of
the Imperial Headquarters Staff. Once more
the dome of St. Sophia, by the sunny Bosphorus,
is the goal of the Colossus of the North—once
more the Turk has to make good his footing in
Europe. Time was when Europe trembled to
see the victorious horse-tails of the Pashas close
under the walls of Vienna. John Sobieski stood
in the gap, and Europe breathed again. Now,
the Ottoman battalions are being hurried to the
Danube, not to threaten, but to defend.

The prologue of the great drama, "The Bulgarian Atrocities," has been played, and the act-drop is down for a while, the audience gnashing their teeth with rage, or grinning with sarcastic sneer, or silent and pale with suppressed excitement. They are deeply moved. All their passions are let loose; race-hatred, religious-hatred, lust for conquest, fear of spoliation, envy, pride, revenge, anger—the whole procession of the Deadly Sins has passed over the stage in the sight of all the world. The interlude on the orchestra is the deep roll of gathering thunder, the increasing roar of the whirlwind, the quaking of earth beneath the drums and tramplings of approaching battalions—a grand and terrible *crescendo*, culminating at length in the trumpet blast which stirs the heart of Holy Russia: "Advance, my children, in God's name!" And now the curtain of the Theatre of the Nations rises for the play.

This little ensuing scene in the first act, in which I am an actor, is a comic scene. Plenty of terrific tragedy follows, of which I shall be a spectator in the front row of the stalls, so to speak, but just now—

> "For me and for my *comedy*,
> Here stooping to your clemency,
> I beg your hearing patiently."

I am the special correspondent of a great newspaper, and have arrived post-haste in Constantinople, accredited to, but discredited by, the Sublime Porte. The newspaper I represent does not love the Sublime Porte; that is a fact with which, as I am soon made aware, the Sublime Porte is painfully familiar. But here I am, amidst the din and the bustle of the preparations for war; the transports, crammed with troops for Varna, are leaving every day, and I must push on at once. I call at the Embassy. The Embassy, as usual, is rather shy of newspaper correspondents, but it is, as usual, extremely polite. I must "go to the Porte and get my pass, then there will be no further difficulty." Not to have the pass means, not the bastinado and the bowstring, but arrest and expulsion from the territories of the Commander of the Faithful.

Rumour says that O'Donovan (poor O'Donovan, of Merv, whose bones lie in the Soudan desert with Hicks's heroes!) has been hustled and worried, and finally arrested and expelled, because he was not amenable to discipline, because he represented a hostile paper, because he was not provided with the necessary permission to go about the country in war time. To be shown out of the country before a shot had been fired? Never! Off I go, across the bridge, to Stamboul and the Porte, and my card is taken to K—— Effendi. " Be pleased to walk this way; be seated." Coffee, cigarettes.

" You have just arrived ? "

" Just arrived, Effendi, and I want to get up to the front as soon as possible."

" Ah! yes; you want your pass—the permission to accompany the Headquarters ? "

" Yes, Effendi."

" One moment." And the Effendi goes to a side table covered with newspapers, gets out one of them, looks at it, and then comes across to me.

" This is your paper ? "

" It is, Effendi."

" You know this article in it ? "

" I have not yet seen this number."

" Will you read this article ? "  I read it.  It is a leading article advocating, in the most emphatic language, the summary dismemberment of the Turkish Empire, and the assignment of its *disjecta membra*, when hanged, drawn, and quartered, to the executioners of Europe, who have the best claim to them.  The Effendi takes the paper from me and smacks it with the back of his hand.

" So, Monsieur, you expect me to give you a pass to the front, you who represent *this !* " (smack).

I rise to explain : I have nothing to do with the leading articles or the politics of the paper which I represent.  I am simply a correspondent sent out here to follow the fortunes of the Turkish army and to report on them.  It is useless. I cannot go to Varna, but " every facility will be given to me *in Constantinople* to hear what is going on."  This rouses me.

"Effendi, my orders are to proceed at once with the troops to Varna, and I must go."

"But you will not be allowed to stay there without your pass, Monsieur."

"Nevertheless, I must go."

"Comme vous voulez, Monsieur."

And so we part: I go on board the Austrian-Lloyd steamer, which is to sail on the morrow for Varna. In company with us is a great troop-ship full of Turkish infantry. As they pass the Dolma Bagtche Palace on the Bosphorus, the troops swarm on deck and shout their salutation to the Sultan, the Turkish "Ave Caesar, morituri te salutant!

Arrived at Varna, which is the base of operations just now, I join the band of correspondents already there assembled. Alas, poor passless wretch! my brother journalists simply bristle with "bouyourouldous"! I am the only one who has nothing, no official document bigger than a postage-stamp to show. I am an object for hilarity, for insincere commiseration. "One rival the less for us," think they; for is it not certain that the Political Commission (attached to the Headquarters for the special censorship of correspondents) will send me back under arrest (if I would not go peaceably) by the next steamer?

But see, now, how small a world it is, and how the events of our past project themselves into our future.

Among the French journalists at Varna is one whose name is very familiar to me. He represents an important Parisian journal. We talk at dinner—we compare notes. "Why that was my father," says he, "who taught you French, my dear old father!" We became friends forthwith, and I move to the house where my new-found friend lodges.

I tell him of my trouble over that accursed pass. "I must have one, you know, my dear B., for the Political Commission have invited all the correspondents to register themselves and their passes within a fortnight."

"It is an invitation," says B., "which cannot be declined, and most assuredly, mon cher, you

B

must accept it; but (and here he laughs) you don't know Turkey. I do; and I think I can manage your pass, your bouyourouldou—gods! what a word it is—for you."

"But how, my dear B.? how? I am down, with the blackest of marks against me, on the books of the Sublime Porte, and I did not stay a moment longer than I could help in Constantinople after my interview with K—— Effendi, confound him! What could I do but come on at once and take all risks?"

"Yes, yes, quite so. But have you twenty pounds?"

"Twenty pounds, my dear fellow, why of course I have."

"Well, hand them over to me, and let your man go back in the steamer to Constantinople with a letter from me. Your case is a bad one, but I know a man ——" then with a laugh, "I am not sure of success; but lay low, and don't rub the Political Commission the wrong way."

The letter is written, a draft is enclosed, and

my servant is summoned. He is an ex-private of Prussian Uhlans who has been through the campaign of 1866. He has a colossal frame, an impervious countenance, and a lacklustre eye. I engaged him in Constantinople.

"What can you do, Fritz?" said I, when we were making our contract as master and servant.

"I have been a soldier, sir; I do all I'm told."

"You are engaged, Fritz"—and never once in all the trying months that followed did I have cause to regret our quick-concluded compact.

"Fritz, you will go to Constantinople by the steamer this afternoon, deliver this letter, and bring back the answer. It is a private letter, and the answer will be private."

"Yessir."

Anxious days of waiting and hoping! The Political Commission, having evidently received instructions about me from the Porte, are kind enough to treat me with all the courtesy and consideration due to a man whose days are numbered, while my colleagues of the press stand me endless drinks. "For," say they, "ere long we shall see thy face no more."

The steamer returns; with her Fritz, the faithful; and with him an envelope a yard square which he has had some difficulty in keeping "private." We go off, my friend and I, and open the portentous document. "Hey!" says B., "what is it? I don't know this kind of bouyourouldou. It isn't like mine or any one else's, and look what a seal! It's all right I expect, but there's no letter with it (feeling all round the corners of the envelope)—nothing! Don't say a word! Bring it out at the meeting, and don't show it, of course, to a soul."

The eventful day arrives, and I am an object of increased pity. I am even charged with messages to friends in Constantinople. Dear, facetious boys! Some of you will be going back to Constantinople before me, and one of you, alas! we, who remain, will bury ere many weeks are gone.

\* \* \* \* \*

SCENE : *The Chamber of the Political Commission in the entrenched camp of Shumla,
with the Headquarters of Achmet Eyoub
Pasha.    The Political Commission sitting.
Journalists—English, French, American—
sitting.    Coffee and cigarettes circulating.*

Preliminary conversations : The weather, the
quality of the meals at the only restaurant, the
slowness of the Russian advance, the splendid
condition of the Turkish Army.

All talk happily save One who sits apart, silent
and morose, as though under the Shadow of
Impending Fate.

" And now to business, Messieurs," says T——
Bey, " the registration of your passes."    The
names are called from the list.    My *confrères*
step up briskly, show their little narrow slips of
paper with the three or four lines of Turkish
print, and the little blue stamped seal of K——
Effendi, or some other equally responsible
official.

My name is called.

- A broad general smile pervades the assembly. The Bey himself, smiles. "Monsieur Huyshe, votre bouyourouldou? vous l'avez?" I slowly unbutton my coat and hand out the document. The Bey commences to unfold it; it gets bigger and bigger as he goes on unfolding, until it looks like a map of the seat of war on a large scale. Now it is fully displayed, and the eyes of the Head of the Political Commission are fixed on the great gold seal in helpless stare. He hands it to his colleagues. They stare; one of them visibly starts.

"What the dickens is it?" says one of the British journalists, *sotto voce.*

"C'est bien, Monsieur," says the Bey, rising to hand me back the paper. "Your pass for the Headquarters is from His Highness the Brother-in-law of the Sultan."

General chorus: "THE BROTHER-IN-LAW OF THE SULTAN!"

TABLEAU.   CURTAIN.

\*       \*       \*       \*       \*

" I say, boys," said I, when we left, "you've been very good to me, standing me drinks ; now *I'll* stand drinks all round."

Afterwards, in our rooms, B. and I, quite as much surprised as any of them, did several smiles together.

" I told you I knew Turkey," said B.

" Yes, by Jove!" said I, "and I'm glad I knew your father.   But look here, old chap ; this is what beats me—who got the £20 ?

> I've searched in vain from Dan to Beer-
> Sheba to make this mystery clear ;
> But I end with it as I did begin,
> *Who got the whisky-skin ?*"

And the best joke of all was, that whenever during the war I passed the sentries and patrols, and was asked to show my bouyourouldou, the exhibition of that document had the effect of causing the man who challenged me to come to attention and present arms.

# CHAPTER II.

## Alarums—Excursions.

JUNE 21, 1877. A highly excited group of war correspondents are we, in the belvedere of the Islah Hané, the only hotel of Rustchuk. Beneath us the Danube rolls its immense stream. The swollen waters, as they sweep majestically towards the distant Euxine, seem as though they *must* flood that flat, dreary Roumanian shore opposite, and drown out the inhabitants of Giurgevo, yonder little hostile town, about a mile below us. The great river is higher than usual. Here, on our Bulgarian side, the banks are steep; on the other side they are low; and so the summer floods widen the stream on that side chiefly. We and our, as yet, silent batteries completely dominate the country opposite; from our watch tower we can see how the river had spread itself inland, and formed extensive lagoons and flooded the marsh land. That is why, since April, when war was declared two months ago, the Russians, who, we know very well are over there in tens of thousands—horse, foot, and artillery—have not been able to come at us. We have watched them daily, marching and countermarching, watering their horses, and working away at their batteries, from which we infer that they intend to bombard us some day. One of our detached forts, six miles down stream, has even fired at some of their infantry, but no boom of heavy guns has yet rolled across the water. The Russians have made no attempt to come over and fight us; we have seen no sign of boat or pontoon.

"The Danube is with us," said an old Turk to me in the hotel garden last night, "the Moscov cannot come."

"But he will come when the river falls?"

"If Allah wills it."

There are half-a-dozen of us up here in the rickety "watch tower" of the Islah Hané. We have stumbled up the narrow stairs in hot haste, regardless of the breakfast which is spread below; knife and fork have been thrown down, the fried fish is getting cold, the barolo uncorked, the appetizing nip of mastique forgotten.

"What is it? where is it?" shouted those who were half-way up to those who were already at the top.

"Look!—up the river! By Jove, they're going to cross!" Flash after flash, cloud after cloud of dense white smoke burst from a point far up the river; then the roar of siege artillery comes rolling down to us. "It is a battery of big guns covering the passage of the river. Flash! Boom! The town folk run from all sides to the bluffs overhanging the river—the esplanade is crowded with people—the soldiers in our batteries stand to arms. Flash! Boom! One of our foreign colleagues hops about the floor like a pea on a drum, and then precipitates himself downstairs. "He's gone to telegraph full details of the passage of the Danube," says one of our wags. "Fritz," say I to my faithful ex-Uhlan, "run you down quick and saddle the horses, and wait." Fritz descends with elephantine step, and the watch-tower rocks the while.

It will take us an hour to gallop out there, and we must be on the move; but there is nothing *on* the river yet. Yes, there is! See! All glasses are levelled; not a word is spoken; we watch in breathless silence a little ripple behind what looks like a short, thick stick, upright in the water. It is moving rapidly across to our side. "A torpedo boat!" bursts simultaneously from our lips. Down the stairs we go, helter-skelter, pell-mell; we dive into our rooms, and in a moment we are streaming out into the streets, buckling on belts and revolvers, stuffing biscuits and whiskey-flasks into our pockets. Fritz is at the horses' heads. I am up and half way to the town gate before he follows, but he comes presently, an immense cavalry sword (which he never leaves for a moment) swinging and clanking as he pounds along.

"Turn to the right at the gate," shouts Fritz; "it is at Pyrgos that they fight."

"To the right it is, sharp round—hold up, horse!" and now, free of the town, away we go in glorious gallop over the short sward of the down-like country—a fresh dig of the spur for each boom of the guns.

In a twinkling we are at the base of the Levent Tepé, the hill which is crowned by our most powerful outlying fort. On the slopes are the white tents of the garrison. This hillside is always alive with troops, but something more than morning parade or a field day is going on now, for, as we gallop past, three splendid battalions are marching out, completely equipped, overcoats slung, Prussian fashion, over the right shoulder, haversack at the left side. Behind them the mules and pack-horses of the baggage train stream along, and at their right rear trundles a well-horsed battery of shining Krupp guns.

"War at last, Fritz!" say I to the faithful one.

"Krieg!" replies he, with war-dog grin.

We ride past the marching battalions, plump

into a double line of skirmishers well in advance; on our right, close to the river, we see a flanking party moving along parallel to the main body — we are evidently in complete formation to resist a landing. Not so fast now; *we* must not skirmish for the skirmishers; friendly skirmishers in one's rear are as uncomfortable as the enemy in front! At length we get to Pyrgos, and come to a halt on the slope of the high ridge away from the river. The three battalions stack arms and lie down, the skirmishing line sinks prone on the crest, and the staff comes over it to reconnoitre the river. A Major rides up to me and wants to know my business here. My hand is on the document which will instantly produce a salute; but my soft answer turns away wrath, and the Major goes off to attend to his own business, which, indeed, is quite as pressing as mine, for he tells me there is reason to believe the Russians will seize one of the islands close to our shore, and that there will be fighting soon.

Dr. Crookshank, of the Turkish Medical

Service (better known, now, in Egypt), joins
me, and we decide to make a private reconnaissance for ourselves.   Giving the staff a wide
berth we walk along the ridge.   As we go, we
see two more battalions advancing to reinforce
us; their bayonets glitter in the bright sun;
behind them groups of men, who have fallen out,
tired, toil along; orderlies gallop to and fro, and
the Krupp battery, still limbered up, is ready to
come into action at a moment's notice—a
stirring, war-like scene which sets our blood
dancing.

The Russian guns open fire again, and their
sound is now no dull, rolling boom, but a short,
fierce roar, for they are a bare thousand yards
away.   What can they be firing at ?   Not a
shell has struck the ridge yet.   We *must* find
out.

The Doctor and I, clear of the troops, descend
the ridge, and mount the lower one immediately
over the river.   The roar of the guns and the
shriek of the shells is deafening as we ascend;
a big shell strikes the slope and we feel as if we

were assisting at an earthquake. Arriving hot,
breathless with excitement, at the top, we stop
short. The mystery is solved! Immediately
beneath us is the river, and on it, close to the
bank, one of our iron-clad gunboats is steaming
slowly along. On the right is a long, low island,
covered with scrub, on the left another similar
island. The gunboat is steaming from one to the
other. As she appears between the islands
the Russian battery opposite blazes away at her
with 64-pound shells. The Doctor and I have
struck the bank between the islands, and we are
in the immediate line of fire. We immediately
lie down.

There, on the Danube shore, forgetful of
danger, and fascinated by the spectacle, we
watch the duel between the gunboat and the
battery. Plucky little gunboat! One of those
big shells would sink her, or blow her up; but
she comes out from behind one island, steams
solemnly across to the other, the shells dashing
up the water before her—behind her—a few
yards from her hull. The Russian gunners have

her range to a fraction; but they are always
a little too soon or a little too late to stop her.
Now she is just opposite us; a shell passes
between her masts, buries itself in the bank
close beneath us, and then bursts, spluttering
mud and water.

"Rather warm," says the Doctor; "ten feet
higher and ——!"

"Quite so, Doctor;" but I inwardly resolve
next time the gunboat arrives at that same
latitude and longitude to shift a bit. The next
time she comes out, as though tired of being a
mark for admirable target-practice, she changes
her tactics, and heads straight across for the
battery. In mid stream she turns, and pop go
her little guns! then she scuttles back—the big
guns roaring at her and dashing the water about.
("Bad times for the fish," say we.) In the shelter
of the island, again, she hides herself. The
Russian artillerymen let fly at the island now;
and for ten minutes or so we lie watching the
bark and the branches fly, listening to the
peculiar sound of the bursting shells, like the

roar of wind as the wood trembles with tremendous concussions. The duel is evidently over.

A movement on the ridge above now arouses us. Two of our Krupp guns trot on to the crest and unlimber. The Doctor and I lose no time in getting behind them. The guns are trained on the Russian battery with a care that is positively amusing. Every man in each squad sights them. The first shell falls far short. More caressing and coaxing of the guns; the next falls we know not where, but it is evident that our little 12-pounders are of no use for this work. Our big enemy disdains reply. A few more ineffectual shots from us, and then the cannonade ceases, the troops fall in, and we all go home to dinner.

But the mysterious torpedo-boat, what of her? Long before we got out here she had gone back to her own side of the river; but her operations had been highly exciting and amusing. As detailed by an intelligent native, who had been an eye-witness, and who possessed a sense of

c

humour, this is what had happened. A Russian torpedo party had set out from the opposite shore for the purpose of laying torpedoes in the Channel and blocking in our fleet. Their boats and launches having been descried, word was sent into the town, and the gunboat had moved out to check the blockading operation. Hardly had she arrived, when the torpedo-boat shot out from the shore.

"A long, grey boat—you see nothing but the top of her deck and her funnel. She makes straight for the gunboat—terrible confusion on gunboat—the crew run about getting a Krupp gun to point in the direction of the on-coming enemy—bang!—water flies up—boat still coming —bang again! right down into water—spray dashing, everyone shouting—boat now close— gun cannot be depressed enough. Then boat rushes round stern of gunboat and goes off back as fast as she came—bang!—no use; boat gone!" Alfred Jingle himself could not have told the story better!

The torpedo-boat, a "Thorneycroft" or a

"Jarrow," had failed to blow up the gunboat—
that was clear; something had gone wrong with
the unpleasant sort of bowsprit, which, as a rule,
carries death and destruction at the end of it.
But the crew of the gunboat had had a rare
waking up, and next morning they found the
unexploded torpedo sticking to their stern!

Out of this grew the affair we had witnessed—
the march out in battle order, and the artillery
duel—the first excitement we had experienced
since the declaration of war. Soon all was quiet
again, and we resumed our attitude of watching
and waiting. We had not to watch and wait
much longer.

# CHAPTER III.

## 𝕷ong 𝕭owls 𝕬cross the 𝕽iver.

"   .   .   .   .   *The nimble gunner,*
*With linstock now the devilish cannon touches,*
*And down goes all before them.*"

"RUSTCHUK, *May* 10*th*, 1877.

"NOTICE.

"To all subjects of Her Britannic Majesty (and others) at Rust-chuk :—The undersigned hereby notifies to all British subjects that as the towns of Oltenitza and Turtukai are already exchanging shots, the military authorities here have some reason to expect a fire from the opposite side of the Danube, possibly directed upon the Railway Station.

"R. READE,

"*Her Majesty's Consul for the Villayet of the Danube.*"

DEAR OLD READE! Well do we re-member thee, thy burly British good nature, and this sly little joke of thine—"*possibly directed upon the Railway Station*"—the only loop-hole of escape for special correspondents!

36

And the charming *naiveté* of " have some reason
to expect!"    Why, there, right opposite the
Islah Hané Hotel, where we lodge, and thy own
Consulate where the Union Jack flies, a long,
brown line has been seen *growing* day after day
along the river shore—a low, evil-looking bank
with little notches in it.    " Some reason to
expect," quotha !    And only the other night
while we were all talking (as usual) about this
battery, one of our number, a kindly soul, whose
room, No. 20, overlooked the river, made the
following remark to our military attaché, Colonel
Lenox, V.C. :—

" But there are no guns in the battery yet,
Colonel."

" Yes, there are," said the Colonel, " I 've
seen 'em."

Now, the Colonel had a most powerful telescope, the envy of all war correspondents in
Rustchuk.    And so it was that room No. 20
was to let next day, in the morning, quite
early.

Yet for many a long week after the issue of

the Consular Notice (the principal effect of
which was the immediate flight of the Branch
of the Imperial Ottoman Bank and the dislocation
of our financial arrangements) that portentous
battery remained silent.  Our own defences were
in complete order; we bristled with Krupps,
big and little.  But in all those weeks of May
and June not a single shot did we fire to destroy
the symmetry of that earthwork, whose nicks
and angles grew daily neater and neater under
our very eyes.

Watch it!  Yes; we lean on the rail by the
river and watch it by the hour together; some
times we even see long teams dragging the
big guns into it.  But fire at it?  Certainly not.
And why not?  Thou poor Unspeakable One!
bless thy innocent heart!  " Because we, the
Turks, intend Europe to see that we are not
the aggressors in this war; because that battery
is on the Roumanian shore and we are not at
war with Roumania."  The sudden horror which
will come presently; a town stricken into ghastly
heaps as by blasts from hell; flames roaring

skyward; foul dogs mumbling men's bones—
that is what is in store for you, you poor de-
generate creature, with your *bakalum*, "we shall
see," and your *kismet*, "it is destiny." And
your Arbiter, Europe, will say, simply, that
you allowed bolts for your own destruction to be
forged under your noses, and that it is right
and proper that you should be knocked into
smithereens.

But can it be that you, and your Sultan,
huddled up with his harem on the Bosphorus, are
the descendants of the Osmanli who swept like
a hurricane over the breach in the triple wall of
Constantinople four hundred years ago; of that
Muhammed II., who rode at their head through
the blazing town, and struck off with his battle-
axe the bronze serpent-head of the Tripod of
Delphi on the very stadium of Justinian?
Indeed, then, if you are, the time has come for
you to get out, bag and baggage, and make way
for better men.    Give the control of your
batteries for one day to these English strangers
within your gates, this Colonel Lenox and

Captain Chermside, and see what *they* would make of yonder accursed earthwork!

Such was the current philosophy wherewith we beguiled the time in the European quarter of Rustchuk during those weary days. But the Colonel, with that admirable telescope at his eye, could only tell us how things were getting on across the water. "Another siege gun, this morning, gentlemen," he would cheerfully remark at breakfast, as though the arrival of the new-comer was really a matter of unmixed satis-faction, and ought to whet our appetites.

But that Russian or Roumanian earthwork across the river is not the only object which perturbs us. Probably some day it will do con-siderable damage to our property; here, now, is something which positively hurts our feelings. We look out of another window of the hotel, away from the enemy and towards our own fortress. Surely that redoubt up there on the ridge where our own Mushir, Eschreff Pasha, lies encamped, does not show front to the foe. Its embrasures face *us!* What *is* this thing?

We will ride up to the Mushir's and see. He is charmed to see us; produces coffee and cigarettes; after which we go out to see the redoubt. Four field-pieces in position behind an earthwork, every piece trained upon our own town of Rustchuk. Two mitrailleuses are added to the battery while we are there.

"Oh yes!" says one of the officers, "we know perfectly well the houses of the leading Bulgarians in the town, and at the first provocation this battery will open fire. So glad you have come up to see that it is so. *Good* morning."

Wretched town, unhappy Bulgarians, sorely-tried war-correspondents! On the one hand, our own British Consul with his "Russian guns possibly directed" on the railway station; on the other hand, this Turkish artillery officer with his guns certainly directed on the town! Were ever men more completely caught between the Devil and the Deep Sea?

But 'tis a true saying, that familiarity breeds contempt, and as the summer days went by the notched lines on the opposite shore, and the

Mushir's "friendly" redoubt upon our own, became to us as portions of the normal landscape. Jovial Reade's paper bombshell was forgotten; we got tired of staring and wondering; indeed, if I remember aright, it was considered rather bad form to talk about the hostile works, and distinctly bad form to show the slightest excitement with regard to them. And so all through the month of June, our scare having subsided, there was for all of us in Rustchuk a time of *dolce far niente.* Turk or Bulgar, Moslem or Giaour, the whole population basked in the sun together; crowds of idlers formed themselves into picturesque groups on the bluffs overhanging the river, and gazed dreamily into or across the placid stream, whose surface was unbroken save by the long reedy islands; children played in the quiet streets; the milk-seller lingered on his rounds; the orange merchant did an easy, thriving trade. In at the hotel window little birds would flit, uninvited but welcome, and hold twittering conversations on the door-top; the swallows wheeled around the minarets or

skimmed the Danube water, screaming with
shrill joy; no breath of air stirred the leaves or
stiffened the flags of the Consulates. At even-
tide the troops would parade on the hills, and,
in their Eastern manner, thrice salute the setting
sun and the Padisha, the trumpets sounding
between each salute. Then, one by one, the
lights went out and solemn silence descended
upon the fortress and the river. Day after day,
such were our days.

And this Sunday morning, the 24th of June,
is a day so utterly lazy that these loungers by
the shore, who contemplate a grave old Turk
fishing with a net, are hardly stirred into faint
movement when he catches (at the forty-first
dip, carefully counted) a four-inch fish. With
him, when he goes off after this haul, perfectly
satisfied with it, departs our only sign of
activity.

Across the water, in the enemy's country, they
are apparently just as sleepy as we, for the only
moving thing to be seen is an ox-cart, crawling
along the dusty road; the cupolas of the church

of Giurgevo glitter in the sun, but give out no
sound of bell ; the village of Slobosia, nearer to
us, shows no sign of human habitation. It is the
only pretty spot on their flat shore, that village,
for it is quite embosomed in green trees. It is
three in the afternoon, and as we sit here in the
hotel garden, sipping mastique and looking
lazily at the crowd on the esplanade, no one
gives a thought to those quiet woods opposite,
save, perhaps, that their shade must be a pleasant
thing this hot day.

*       *       *       *       *

Thunder ? Surely not ? But we all start to
our feet as a dull, sullen roar breaks upon our
ears. See! in the Slobosia wood, a dense white
cloud! And now, here, above our heads, a shriek
in the air ! The holiday crowd breaks into
chattering, and then, as nothing else happens,
it titters. For a quarter of an hour, laughing,
talking, gesticulating; the white cloud has
vanished; thousands of eyes, bent upon the place
where it was, see nothing—nothing but the same

quiet woods. What was it? Where is it?—a thing devised by the enemy to fright us from our Sunday rest?——

Now, swift and sudden, not one peal but twenty terrific thunder-bursts. That accursed wood gapes on us like the mouth of hell; flames burst from it; its cloud-pall is riven by darting tongues of flame and fire; the air above us is full of shrieks as of lost souls driven in torment through the sky; the very sunlight has become dun and livid; the thundering roar that comes across the water is echoed, here, among us, by dull crashes.

A frenzied shout, " THE BOMBARDMENT ! THE BOMBARDMENT !" then a terrible panic. Mad with terror, the crowd rushes for the cover of houses and walls; the streets swarm with a screaming throng of men, women, and children. " They are firing on the town, not on the forts," is now the cry as the terrified mass struggles along, the strong treading down the weak in the flight for safety. Safety! Where? For the whole town now resounds with infernal din;

houses, smitten by sudden bolts, are dashed to
pieces; their roofs become the edges of yawning
chasms; minarets totter to their fall; clouds of
dust fill the streets; stones and tiles whizz in the
air; masses of rending iron hum their fatal
death-song as the great shells burst in the open
squares. A pitiless hail! " Away from the town!
Away from the town !" Horses are saddled and
harnessed, and lashed into mad gallop. In every
quarter, Turks, Bulgars, Jews, snatch up their
children, their money, such possessions as they
can carry, and swell the stream of fugitives.
They are caught by the storm and dashed to
death—fifty and more of them—ere they can get
clear of the crashing streets. Hour after hour
the iron hail beats upon defenceless roofs; yet
many of the poorer inhabitants cling to their
homes, huddle into corners and await their fate.
They are as safe there as in the street. Real
safety is to be found only on the bare hill-side.

There, among the vineyards, what a sight is to
be seen! The whole of *our* batteries have
opened fire; *our* shore reels with the din of

answering cannon. Down below our standpoint our houses fall with thundering crash ; over yonder we can see that *their* houses reel, totter, and disappear. We are doing for Giurgevo what Giurgevo is doing for us—giving tit for tat! No, not quite. These Moslem artillery-men are not firing upon that building yonder, over which a white flag flies. And our hospitals, over which also the white flags were flying this afternoon, what of them ?

In the midst of terror and panic our doctors, Crookshank, Stivens, and Roy, and their assis-tants, have hastily carried out the sick and feeble and placed them on mattresses in the open square. With good cause for haste, for our white flags were shot away in the first hour, and the buildings beneath them stare open to the sky.

And so the sun went down that Sunday even-ing, hailed, as usual, by paraded troops and sound of trumpet. In the thrice-repeated shouting there is a tone which tells of deeper, fiercer hate for the Christian who had fired upon helpless men, and buildings marked out for mercy by the flag of the Geneva Convention; for a Russian shell has actually fallen through the roof of our hospital, fired, the Turks say, with deliberate aim and intent. But they are so anxious for a set-off to those "atrocities" at Batak!

.

# CHAPTER IV.

## Rustchuk in Ruins.

*"I'd play incessantly upon these jades,*
*Even until unfenced desolation*
*Leaves them as naked as the vulgar air."*

TURKISH OFFICIAL DESPATCH.—" The Russians, defying the right of humanity, and without any military necessity, have completely destroyed the flourishing town of Rustchuk, which is now nothing but a heap of ruins, by directing their fire especially upon habitations outside the fortifications and our works of defence.  The Russian army has spared neither the religious edifices, the hospitals, nor the public buildings, and has thus carried out a work destitute of all justification, and which has no object but devastation.  For this reason we hereby make it known to the justice and humanity of Europe and the public conscience."

SUCH was the appeal of the Turk, sent forth immediately after that terrific opening day of the bombardment.  But unfortunately the "justice and humanity of Europe and the public conscience" had not yet recovered from the

shock of the *Turkish* atrocities at Batak.
Barely six weeks before the Russian batteries
opened fire Ambassador Layard had been compelled to remind the Sublime Porte that Chefket
Pasha—Chefket, the Batak butcher—was still in
Europe, and that his presence was a desecration
to European soil. And we had seen Chefket
passing like the shadow of a black cloud over
the peaceful Bulgarian landscape, hurried off by
train to an Asiatic post, where he might cut
Christian throats without so much fuss being
made about the matter. But the real reply to
the Russian bombardment took the distinctly
practical form of sending 700 shells per diem
into the town of Giurgevo. Reading afterwards
in the papers the account of a correspondent on
the Russian side, we dwelt with satisfaction upon
his statement that the town was so knocked
about that he couldn't find on Monday the
restaurant in which he had dined on Sunday.
We read, too, that the inhabitants had been
driven to take refuge in bough huts, amid rain
and misery; we wondered not a little to read

that many of our shells did not explode because they were filled with *coal dust* (merciful contractor!); and we smiled grimly when we saw that our bombardment of Giurgevo was spoken of as a "wanton attack upon an open town."

Yet, even in the very heat of the cannonade the Turkish authorities kept up their remarkable determination not to hit first. "See," they said to the consuls, "the Russian fire is directed upon our mosques; we will now fire upon the church of Giurgevo." And away went the shells from the seven-ton Krupp at the Christian domes! The dome of the great church of Giurgevo was indeed quite a handsome mark for us, but what shall be said of the artillery practice of the Russian gunners? One often hears of some crack pistol shot who can snuff his candle at so many paces, but here was the mosque at the corner of the great square with the extinguisher-shaped top of its minaret taken clean off at 3,000 yards with a 64-pound shell!

And they made quite as good practice at poor dear old Consul Reade's flagstaff. The British-

American Consulate was situated on the river shore, and on its flagstaff the Union Jack was ever a pleasant sight to us English, as it fluttered a-top. Among the very first of the big shells which came roaring across the water, one crashed into Mr. Reade's roof, exploded in his bedroom, and blew out the upper corner of the house. "They are firing at your flag—at our flag—at the Union Jack!" was the English cry; "hoist the larger one, Mr. Reade, they will see that." Reade was not a man to haul down his flag under any circumstances, but there was common sense in this, so down came the small Union Jack, and up went one which was eighteen feet by nine. "They can see what *that* is, surely." A few moments of suspense. Then, from the same battery, crash! comes a shell through the front wall. Ten minutes after, another, which bursts in the study, reduces the whole of the furniture to matchwood; desks, chairs, boxes vanish under three feet of bricks and plaster, and a big splinter goes through the Queen's Proclamation over the door. "It is evident,"

ROUGH TIMES FOR THE "SPECIALS."

A BOMBARDED MOSQUE.
(*Drawn by the Author.*)

says the French Consul, "that they are firing at your house, and I must implore you to come away." And so the British Consul reluctantly leaves his shattered residence, and the 18 by 9 Jack waves no more. Not long after, the turn of the French Consul arrived ; his roof was missing one afternoon, and an unexploded eight-inch shell stuck in the wall of his bedroom, as ocular evidence that they had fired at *his* house. With neat precision a big sixty-four pounder plumped on the roof of the Consulate of Austria, and crashed through three floors of the house, wrecking the rooms it passed through. And here was a queer thing! In the pretty sitting-room, in the corner close to where the shell had descended, was a bowl of gold fish — the bowl uncracked and the fish swimming merrily about!

A ramble through the desolated town in the intervals of the cannonade revealed strange sights. With what grim satisfaction did we stand and contemplate the ruins of the Pasha's palace ? In the latter days of the bombardment even the ruins of it had perished, and we could stand upon the heap of rubbish which marked the site of the room from which, after weary waitings and comings again, we had so often been politely bowed out with the assurance that "His Excellency, the Vali, was asleep on his divan, and could not be disturbed," or that "His Excellency's rheumatism really prevented his seeing any one that morning." Alas! a few nicely calculated flights of six and eight-inch shells had driven His Excellency from his divan, and even the rheumatism from His Excellency. Where *was* His Excellency? Out there on the bare hillside in a tent!

Here, in this square, where the Pasha's residence, the hospitals, and the telegraph offices stood, the scene on the first day of the bombardment was one of indescribable terror and confusion. No one had dreamed of danger, for did not the white flag with the red crescent fly over three hospitals? By the 28th June seventy shells had fallen in the quarter, and the military, civilian, and orphans' hospitals had

THE BRITISH CONSULATE, RUSTCHUK, UNDER FIRE.

THE CONSULATE AFTER A VISIT FROM A 64 POUND SHELL.

become heaps of ruin. Before the doctors had time to rescue the patients on that terrible Sunday, a bomb came through the roof of one of the hospitals, and burst on the floor between the rows of beds without hurting a man! Outside in the square, men, women, and children were rushing for cover like rabbits to their holes; the Turkish women, alone disdaining to run, shuffled slowly across the open space with startled eyes glaring over their yashmaks. In the midst of the crash of roofs and the roar of bursting shells the doctors—all honour to them—regardless of personal danger, were getting out mattresses and ambulances, and moving their helpless patients (those who were not quite helpless moving themselves with remarkable alacrity) to the place of safety, the hill-side. " To your tents, O Israel!" Happy those who had such shelter!

Day after day the Russian batteries beat upon the town, and it soon became evident that the bombardment was to be conducted on a regular system. Every afternoon when the sun began to decline, and the light was favourable for accurate practice, the siege guns opened fire. Regularly at five in the afternoon there was a three hours' cannonade, watched with painful interest by the wretched inhabitants camped on the hills. At nightfall they would creep down and enter the town, some to sleep in their houses and hovels, others to work all night moving their goods and chattels, others to find that they were homeless. How many wretched beings were actually killed in their homes was never known. The Jews suffered most in this way; the houses in their quarter had no cellars, and many who could not bring themselves to abandon all they had were buried beneath their own roofs.

The Bulgarians, too, suffered severely at the hands of their liberating friends, and many paid with their lives and property for the privilege of being " protected " by so great a Power. For the time they were content to be protected by their enemy. Poor Bulgars ! After being massacred by the Turk owing to the protection of Russia, they were now being cut to pieces by

Russia and protected by the Turk. Their very church was knocked to pieces, and a Catholic church, over the door of which was the motto "Venite Exultemus," shared the same fate. A shell, bursting inside, shook the very altar into ruin. Well might the Turk exclaim, "How these Christians love one another!"

Hardly since the days of Sebastopol can such a sight have been witnessed as this bombardment of Rustchuk. Viewed from the ridge on which the Marshal's camp was pitched, it was a spectacle at once terrible and sublime. The Marshal obligingly gave us full permission to lie in the trenches near his tents, and to be fired at by the Russian sixty-fours. From the heights a splendid view of the whole town, the Danube, and the opposite shore could be obtained, and the flight of the shells could be traced as they came screaming across the river, and found their billet in house or hospital. We could hear the dull rattling crash and see clouds of dust and smoke rise up, as the shells exploded, smashing tiles, and rafters, and walls. The camp and its fortifications were also under fire. As we lay in the trenches the ground about us would be suddenly scooped by a shell, and we would duck under the level of the ground, while the shattered iron flew singing over us. There was but little harm done out there in the open, and even the most "cautious" war-correspondent got to look upon shell fire, under these circumstances, with equanimity. In the town it was quite another thing, and when we were caught there by the bombardment it was a matter of life and death to get out as soon as possible.

On the fourth day of the bombardment the whole town was caught napping, and, as I happened to be one of the crowd, I witnessed another scene of panic similar to that of the first day. We had already got accustomed to the five o'clock opening of the fire, and we had, as usual, strung up our nerves for that hour. The town was full of people, packing up their wretched goods and chattels in a sad and half-hearted but leisurely sort of way; they thought they had the whole morning at least before them.

Suddenly, at nine o'clock, without any warning, the Russian batteries open fire; the Turkish guns immediately respond. The air is alive with the shrieking of shells ; the ground trembles with the thunder of heavy guns. A desperate stampede ensues ; men, women, children, horses, mules, oxen, a dense struggling mass, flee up the streets to the back of the town.

My soldier servant and I mount and ride along with the torrent as steadily and slowly as possible. *We* cannot afford to be panic-struck. He is a soldier, and I an Englishman among foreigners. We rein up under a wall to watch the scene of terror and confusion, but a big 64-pound shell bursts just the other side, and we are spattered with pebbles and plaster; our horses plunge, and kick, and rear; we must go on. Here is a sight! one of the shells has burst in the street, and the dead are lying about; not men in uniform, with arms in their hands, but wretched townsfolk, poor villagers, and here—merciful Heaven !—here is a woman killed by a splinter, and her little child

E

lies beside her, both its legs torn off. The frantic crowd passes them, and other sights as ghastly, without pause. So dense is it, and so mixed up, that it is barely possible to distinguish individuals, but I remember—with a smile, now—some of the quaint figures of that fugitive throng; a small man, for instance, who has an immense pole on his shoulder, to each end of which are hung baskets, bottles, jars, and pans in such number that the pole bends and the loads bob up and down with destructive clatter as the poor little fellow runs.

A grand old Turk, too, remains in my mind; white-bearded, with immense turban, and a sash full of pistols and knives; with him are his three wives—bundles of calico, with pairs of eyes visible near the top—and, in the hand of each, delightful little bare-legged children. And the whole party trots—that is the only word—steadily up the street, uttering no sound of lamentation as do those Bulgar vassals, no weeping and wailing—absolute silence and a steady trot.

PLAN OF THE RUSSIAN & TURKISH BATTERIES BY WHICH RUSTCHUK & GIURGEVO WERE RESPECTIVELY BOMBARDED.

LAKE OF
BALTA MAIZA

Slobosia
*Village*

Woods masking the
Batteries

Thickly wooded Island masking
the Batteries

RUSTCHUK

R I V E R   D A N U B E

Island

Giurgevo

Church

Russian line of fire ----
Turkish line of fire ----

ROAD

Vineyards

And so, amid ceaseless roar of cannon and crashing of shells, which shatter roofs and walls, and send the window shutters flying in splinters along the street, the struggling crowd, leaving many of its number lying on the roadway—poor fragments of mortality, looking like huddled-up heaps of clothes as they lie there—gains once more the hillside and the vineyards. But this cruel, *morning* bombardment has convinced the inhabitants that the Russians mean to make war in the direst and fiercest fashion, and they finally abandon the town. It is impossible to live camped out there on the bare hill, and the majority of the population flees by rail to Rasgrad, and Shumla, and Varna.

\*    \*    \*    \*    \*

Some days afterwards I visited Rustchuk. I found under the burning July sun a city crumbling to ruins. An immense fire had destroyed all that remained of the public buildings; in the Turkish and Jewish quarters mosque and hovel were mingled in heaps of ruin; the fœtid air told of what lay beneath; the streets were silent as a churchyard; here and there some wretched creature crouched among the ruins, looking for his home, may be, or for what was once dearer than home; lean hungry dogs skulked about gnawing and snarling over hideous fragments; overhead, thousands of crows wheeled in the air. I left the town at sunset—a glowing, crimson sunset which seemed to steep the ruins in blood. On the riverside I came upon a strange weird figure, a woman, a Turkish woman, with lank drapery, the ghostly-looking yashmak veiling her face and head; there on the bank, grey and gaunt, she stood, and, looking across the river, with outstretched arms she shrieked out what seemed like some terrific incantation. "What is the matter with this woman?" I asked the sentry, as I passed out at the postern. "She is mad, Effendi; she has lost her reason. Her house and her people have been destroyed in the bombardment. She goes up there on the bank at sunset every evening to curse the Moscov Giaour."

# CHAPTER V.

## The Passage of the Danube.

"Let us preserve every stone of our fortresses, every inch of our territory, which has been purchased at the price of the blood of our ancestors or brothers, who fell conquerors or martyrs. As long as our troops fulfil their sacred duties, the divine grace and spiritual assistance of the Prophet will guide. Your Sovereign will always be with you, and will be ready, if need be, to unfurl the Sacred Banner of the Khalifate and Sultanate, and to sacrifice his life for the honour, the rights, and the independence of our country."—*The Sultan to his Army*, April, 1877.

IT was well said, your Majesty! All along the great river, in these latter days of June, the Russian batteries, planted on the Roumanian bank, have been bombarding your vassal-state of Bulgaria. For three days the cannon-thunder has echoed along the banks, from Widdin on the Servian frontier to Ibraïla, and the Black Sea shore. Rustchuk, your great Danubian fortress, is in ruins; Nicopolis is blazing; Widdin and

Turtukai have been well-nigh knocked to pieces ; and, during these three days of bombarding and battering, the commander of the Ottoman armies, concentrated in the strongholds which have been so roughly used, does not seem to have the remotest inkling where the invaders would attempt the passage of the river. Yet, for weeks before the bombardment the river was falling, the lagoons on the other side were rapidly drying up, and it was certain that the enemy *would* cross.

And now the news runs like wildfire throughout Bulgaria, and along the telegraph wire to the Palace on the Bosphorus, that, in the midst of that general bombardment, so incessant, so fierce, so perplexing, the Russians *had* crossed the Danube—crossed, and landed, and fixed themselves on our bank. Now for the Sacred Banner, now for your Majesty's sword, and—*væ victis !*

But what is this? "*The passage of the Danube by the Russians causes no uneasiness in Turkish military quarters.*" Indeed?

"Messieurs ·the Correspondents, you will be good enough to advise your respective journals that the passage of the river causes no uneasiness in Turkish military quarters."

" By all means, Messieurs the Political Commission," said we, "and delighted we are to hear it.   Doubtless the Commander-in-Chief has his plan of campaign ready ? "

" Messieurs, he has his plan."

If the main feature of his plan was to allow 120,000 men to establish themselves, with trifling loss, on the Turkish side of the river, and to remain unmolested during the ten days of the operation, it was a successful plan.   But we never knew more of it, for within three weeks Abdul Kerim and his plan went back to Constantinople, and were no more seen or heard of.   Excellent old man !   A genuine " old " Turk ; affable, imperturbable, and, like Joey B., devilish sly.

" What I want, Excellency," said one of my colleagues to him once, in a gush of martial ardour ; "what I want is to see the heaviest of the fighting."

" Very well," said Abdul, with a gracious smile, "then you must stay with me."

Abdul did not like war correspondents to go about the country prospecting for war news, and here was one, at least, who walked straight into his net. 'Cute old man!

Sixteen gunboats and monitors on the Danube; 30,000 fighting men of the first quality at Rust-chuk; as many, and as fine, at Widdin; garrisons at Sistova and Nicopolis, in touch with the two main bodies on either side.—surely such a force, concentrating, converging, and then striking with all their might, will sweep the Russian *tête-de-pont*—bridge there was none as yet—it was all head and no body—into the river? So said we. Alas! where *are* the warships? Scattered all along the river; two here, two there, four water-bound somewhere down stream, one (surrounded by torpedoes and checkmated) somewhere else; but at the place were they were wanted, and at the time when they were wanted—not one! Even now, could the eleven which are *not* water-bound, or blockaded, come steaming along to Sistova, they could smash up these boat loads of Russians which keep crossing, and prevent the bridge being made, while the armies of Rustchuk and Widdin, marching towards each other, could grind the Moscov to powder as between two mighty millstones. Vain hope! That is what *might* have been.

A prettier little town than Sistova is not to be met with anywhere along the Bulgarian shore of the Danube; a sunshiny little town, partly nestling in a hollow between the low cliffs, partly straggling out of the hollow on to the higher ground around it. Behind are ridges covered with gardens and vineyards, and behind them again a higher ridge, bare and down-like, but pleasing in its soft undulations and gentle contours. A pleasant little place, which must look like a paradise to the people on the opposite bank, at Simnitza. No vineyards and gardens there, no swelling upland, nothing but flat swamp, half mud, half meadow, half sand, broken only by a wood of willow and alder not far below the town. A dreary shore! But what is going on there, this dark night of the 26th of June? The mud flats are alive! All night long men march on to them, floundering in the darkness, slowly winding along the treacherous track, but gathering surely, hour by hour, behind the willow wood in great black masses. It is Dragomiroff's division and the 4th Rifle Brigade—fully fifteen thousand men in heavy marching order.

A dark night! But these swarming thousands are busy. Well they may be, for they have with them the whole pontoon train of the Russian army, 100 boats and rafts, 16 mountain guns, and 40 field pieces. And their secret orders are to cross the river, here, to-night. The Archduke Nicholas has so decided. He will take no denial. The river shall run red, perhaps; but it must be crossed. Yonder little bay, below Sistova, where a tiny river falls into the Danube, is the place of landing. There is a Turkish camp above it, and a battery of guns. Camp and battery must be stormed. Those are Dragomiroff's orders, and Dragomiroff sets to work to carry them out.

A dark night! But the boats are launched in a creek, then hauled out into the stream. The pontonnier battalions man them, and by midnight they are ready to embark the advance guard, the "forlorn hope" of the Danube. Meanwhile the forty field-pieces are dragged to the river-side, and placed in position to cover the passage. Twelve companies of the Volhynia and Minsk regiments of infantry enter the boats; their General, Yolchine, pushes off and leads the way; the little flotilla follows. Will they catch the Turks napping over there? As the day breaks a spattering fire announces that the boats have been seen. The twelve companies land, and Yolchine instantly orders them to lie down. Down they go on the muddy shore, and in another moment they are skirmishing in the dim light, shot for shot, with the Turkish outposts. A stream of boats is coming over to help them to hold their ground. But now the Turks are wide awake. Both sides of the river burst into flame and smoke; the Russian batteries open fire; the Turkish shells come plunging and splashing into the river and into the willow copse. There is half an army corps as a mark for them there, and can it be possible that the fleet of boats can escape being hit? What a terrible result a single shell crashing into one of those boats will have! Still they put out from the shore and keep crossing, each with its load of forty men; every moment Yolchine's little band gets bigger and its fire fiercer. Broad daylight now, and alas! a shell smashes into one of the boats which contains two guns, their gunners, and the commander of the battery. They perish to a man, torn by the shell, drowned in the river.

But see! Yolchine is strong enough to attack; he gives the word to advance. With a cheer the companies of the Volhynia and Minsk dash at the Turkish line and drive it back. The battery behind it limbers up and retires. Dragomiroff himself has come over now with fifteen companies more, and the lower ridge is gained. Still the boats arrive and disembark their loads, till hundreds have become thousands, and the Turkish guns, though manfully fought, are silenced by that terrible row of nine-pounders on the Simnitza shore.

By eleven o'clock two whole brigades are safe over, and a general advance upon the heights behind the town is ordered.

The heights are gained after a feeble resistance. All that the 5,000 Turks who were encamped there were capable of doing has been done, and now they are in full retreat, some to Rustchuk, some to Nicopolis. The victorious Russians look down into Bulgaria from the crest of the high ridge—Sistova is theirs, and the mighty Danube flows, conquered, behind them! By nightfall twenty-five thousand men are in a defensible position, and the first line of defence of the Turkish Empire in Europe is lost.

By the 28th another Russian division had settled down on the heights of Sistova, and the construction of the bridge was commenced.

On the 2nd July the bridge was ready, and fresh thousands poured over—horse, foot, and artillery.

And what was the splendid garrison of Rustchuk—one day's march away—doing all this time?

F

They paraded every evening; saluted the setting sun with their thrice-repeated cheer and the sound of bugles.

And their commander, Abdul Kerim, fine old Turk, what was he doing?

Thinking over his "plan," no doubt; but eating, mostly.

# CHAPTER VI.

## Ave, Caesar, Liberator!

"My troops have crossed the Danube. To-day they enter your territory, where they have already several times fought for the amelioration of the lot of the Christian inhabitants of the Balkan Peninsula. I have confided to my Army, commanded by my brother, the Grand Duke Nicholas, the mission of securing the sacred rights of your nationality. These rights you have acquired as the reward of centuries of suffering, and of the martyrs' blood with which you and your forefathers have for centuries soaked the soil of your country. Inhabitants of Bulgaria! Russia's object is to build up and not to destroy. The life, liberty, honour, and property of every Christian will be equally guaranteed. Bulgarians! you are passing through a memorable period; the hour of deliverance from Mussulman tyranny has at last struck. With humility, I pray our Lord to grant us the victory over the enemies of Christianity, and to send down His blessing upon our just cause."

SO spake the Czar. The Danube is bridged; the Army of Liberation has passed over—horse, foot, and artillery—and stands on Bulgarian soil; stands so firm, so confident, that the idea of driving it back across the river seems now like a

foolish dream.   The Balkans, the second line of
the defences of Constantinople, lie in front, no
enemy intervening ; already a cloud of Cossacks
spreads over Central Bulgaria, up to the very foot
of the mountains, within sight of Tirnova, ancient
capital of Sclavonian Kings.   What is to hinder
the invading host from marching straight on and
seizing the passes ?   Nothing (for a while) *does*
hinder impetuous Gourko ; he does go straight
on, with eight regiments of horse, six battalions
of tirailleurs ; reconnoitres on his left flank ; finds
out all he wants to know in that direction; then,
pushing through the passes, led by Christian
guides and by Prince Tserteleff disguised as a
Bulgarian peasant, he defeats dribbling reinforcements sent up by the Turks, occupies their
empty earthworks, descends into the plain.
There stands Sulieman with a large army, and
Gourko has to go back, fighting desperately, but
he seizes and holds the Schipka Pass, against
which, later, Sulieman dashes himself in vain.
A romantic raid, worthy of Stonewall Jackson !

From Gourko's headquarters news goes back

to the Czar, which tells him what kind of an
enemy it is whom, at last, the Russian troops
have met. The news lashes the Christian host
into fury. What is it that this group of mounted
staff officers are standing round, bareheaded and
silent? A heap of naked, headless corpses, once
men who wore the Russian uniform and fought
bravely. Those who were killed outright and
those who were only wounded—all alike are
headless. And there are other mutilations of
which no word can be spoken.

Another heap near by—what is it? Heads,
which once belonged to those poor gashed trunks,
and beside them our English Brackenbury
sketching them! The murder and mutilation
of helpless wounded men—this, then, is to be
one of the terrors of the War of Liberation!—
this a part of the burden which the Czar must
bear that Bulgaria may shake off the yoke! Yes,
this, everywhere; in the Balkans, on the Lom,
on the glacis of the Plevna redoubts.

" Bloodthirsty savages outside the pale of civil-
isation."—" Giaours and unbelievers, foes of the

Prophet, ever scheming injury to the true faith.
Heaven opens to our warriors who die fighting
you.   Heaven smiles at the desecration of the
carcases of infidel dogs."

So it has always been since Cross met Crescent
in battle ; so it will always be.   Years after, in
the Soudan desert, I was to see the same hideous
sights ; then, alas! they were English bodies
on which the bloody vengeance of Islam was
wreaked ;   the   same   remorseless   vengeance
wreaked in precisely the same manner.   The
subject of the Sultan and the follower of the
Mahdi were united by the same bond—the "true
faith."   Sober, temperate, dignified men in time
of peace; furious assassins and cowardly butchers
in time of war—Religion, the transforming power!

So, mingled with joy and admiration for
Gourko's bold ride, came the terrible revelation :
" No quarter."   War to the knife, then, until
Bulgaria is freed from this cut-throat horde.
Hail! Alexander, Liberator !

. " The Royal Family of Russia," wrote one of
my colleagues, who followed the fortunes of the

THE PRICE OF VICTORY.

Russian army, "do not spare themselves when the other subjects of the Czar are exposed upon the battle-field. In Russia it is not the fashion that lofty station gives exemption from more dangerous tasks of patriotism." *Noblesse oblige.* And here, now, in the first days of July, this little Danubian town of Sistova is honoured with the presence of the Czar, the Czarewitch, the Grand Duke Nicholas; Princes and nobles of the Empire are here also; and all these personages, Imperial, Princely, noble, are on active service with the Russian armies—a lesson to the commander of the Faithful, who has talked, to be sure, about "unfurling the Sacred Banner" and "leading his troops to victory or death," but upon whom no Ottoman soldier has yet set eyes in the field. He is still huddled up with his harem at Dolma Bagtche.

Everywhere the Bulgarians, wild with enthusiasm, hail the Czar; everywhere, at the same time, they sack and pillage the quarters of the flying Turks. The Turkish quarter of Sistova is a wreck; the interiors of the houses torn to pieces, furniture smashed, divans ripped, windows knocked out; the very floors torn up in the search for treasure. Mosques are ruined, their very railings broken into small pieces. Such was the revenge of Bulgarian Sistova for centuries of Turkish rule, and the annual surrender of eighty per cent. of its industries.

But now the news comes that the Czar is crossing the river, and the Bulgarians of Sistova make ready to welcome him. They discard the red Turkish fez for a white one. No more cowering now beneath the Crescent! On their arms the Bulgars wear a white armlet, on which is a golden Cross; joy is in their faces, welcome on their lips.

Every man of the army that has crossed the Danube is a hero. The three divisions and the Rifle Brigade are paraded to greet the Emperor; to gallant Yolchine's Brigade—the first to make the passage—falls the high honour of lining the road which leads into the town. The Czar arrives; his first act is to embrace Dragomiroff, the hero of the crossing, and to decorate him

ALEXANDER II., CZAR OF ALL THE RUSSIAS.

with the Cross of St. George. Thanks, then,
and praise to his brave soldiers, and he moves on
to the town. A Bulgarian priest awaits him at
the entrance; the Czar kisses the cross and
tastes the bread and salt. Women and children
swarm in the street, and strew his path with
flowers. In the church a Te Deum is sung and
the Sacrament taken. Sistova has never seen
such a day, and the Liberator returns to the
Roumanian shore, well pleased and happy.

And the next move? A triumphal march, led
by Grand Duke Nicholas, to Tirnova, the
ancient capital. Amid cheers and blessings,
handshakings and tears, the women and girls
bring fresh spring water for the thirsty soldiers;
fruits and flowers are showered upon them.
Arches of green boughs span the approaches of
the villages; the soldiers uncover as they pass
through. Processions of priests come out to
meet the advancing host, with banners and
pictures, singing as they come. Near Tirnova,
two ancient monasteries send forth their monks
with a Bible, which the soldiers kiss. Most

affecting sight of all, the monks hoist up to the belfry bells which for four hundred years have lain hidden and silent. Soon the little valley peals with the glad sound.

The muezzin shall call no more from the minaret, but, in his place, the Christian bell shall summon to prayer. There are no bounds to the joy. Four hundred years of cowering slavery to Islam, and now, on this July day of 1877, the Cross and the Bible taken out in procession into the free air, with thousands of armed men around them, ready to give their lives that it shall be so, henceforth! From the Danube to the Balkans, along a broad belt through the centre of Bulgaria the Cross is raised triumphant, and it seems that all the liberators have to do is march on, over the mountains, lowering the Crescent as they go, until St. Sophia is in sight.

Who would have thought, in those early days of July, that the line of that triumphal march from the river to the Balkans would have to be held by the sacrifice of 50,000 lives, and that, months from now, so far from marching through the mountains upon Constantinople, the whole power of Russia would be concentrated upon the siege and capture of a fortified village? Yet, even while the monastery bells were beginning to ring in the gorge of Tirnova, Osman of Widdin, quick to see and bold to venture, had come out, advanced upon the Russian right flank, seized Plevna, and planted himself there. From the fortifications, which rose as by magic at his bidding, these regiments of the Cross now pelted so playfully and prettily by women and girls with flowers and fruit, were to be mown down like grass by a hail of bullets, their shattered remnants driven in headlong rout down the slopes, withered, shrivelled, annihilated by the deadly blast.

But just now there is little heed of Osman, very little knowledge, indeed, of him or of Plevna. The Christian army is in Bulgaria, and the Czar himself has trodden Bulgarian ground. That is enough! "AVE, CAESAR, LIBERATOR!"

# CHAPTER VII.

## Plevna.

*As whence the sun 'gins his reflection,*
*Shipwrecking storms and direful thunders break;*
*So, from that spring whence comfort seem'd to come,*
*Discomfort swells.*                    MACBETH.

IF ever people lived in a fool's paradise, the
Russian armies did so, during those halcyon
days in the month of July, 1877, when their path
through Bulgaria was strewed with flowers and
blessed by priests. For nearly three weeks after
the passage of the river hardly a shot was fired
(there was no tangible enemy to fire at), and the
military operation of lining a lane for the main
body to march through was performed with
leisurely tranquillity. The Czarevitch's army—
the 12th and 13th corps—faced the Turkish army
of Rustchuk. Krüdener, with the 9th corps,
turned off in the opposite direction to Nicopolis.

Between these two, thus guarding the lane, back to back, the main army, pioneered by Gourko, who held the Schipka Pass, was to advance and burst through the Balkan barrier. Each of the three sections set about its business with a light heart.

The special correspondents with the Russian host bore witness to the charming ease of the task. "All concern regarding the passage of the Balkans may be dismissed." "With our knowledge of the whereabouts of the mass of the Turkish army, the date of the arrival of the Russians in Adrianople becomes merely a question of marching and of supplies." Another, speaking of the capture of Nicopolis, says, " The gain of the fortress frees the Russians from the threat of attack on their right flank." Gallant Hassan, who defended Nicopolis with desperate bravery, has been brought in a prisoner, and bears himself with calm self-possession in the presence of Caesar. "It is a stupid war," he says, "into which England has led Turkey," and he for one will be glad when it is over. Off goes

G

Hassan into honourable captivity in Roumania, and Nicopolis troubles his Majesty no more. The cavalry have scoured the country up to Rustchuk on the left, up to Plevna on the right, up to the Balkans in front, and "there has been no opposition worthy of the name." "The Russians," wrote another correspondent, "seem to have put all their eggs into the basket which they have so successfully carried across the Balkans, and it seems pretty certain they will carry the eggs unbroken into Adrianople."

But what is this news, this cloud, no bigger than a man's hand, which breaks the even tint of the clear sky with a splotch of ugly grey? When Krüdener went against Nicopolis he did not think it worth while to protect his flank by occupying PLEVNA, a mere open village, though he soon became aware that there were Turks there. Turks in Plevna? Turn them out! And three regiments undertook to do it. They skirmished themselves into the village; then, laying aside their packs, straggled about, singing. The cavalry did not patrol further—what was the use? Plevna was not of much account anyhow, and were they not in possession? Suddenly, to the extreme surprise of the three jolly regiments, they found themselves being forcibly ejected from Plevna. Ejected! By Heaven! beset on all sides, ringed round with volleys, fighting for dear life! Nearly three thousand men paid the penalty: the wounded were slaughtered to a man; the survivors had to run for it, else the whole three regiments would have been simply swallowed. Clearly the basket of eggs has had a good shake! This little matter must be set right; Plevna must be smashed. A cavalry brigade and an infantry brigade are detached from Prince Schakofskoy's force on the east and marched off to the west, the Prince going with them; a division of the 4th corps, crossing the river and making for Tirnova, is also ordered to march Plevna-wards, and the 9th corps, flushed with victory at Nicopolis, also converges upon the troublesome village. Plevna certainly *will* be smashed! Krüdener and Schakofskoy make their arrangements, and Skobeleff will help; their

entire force will concentrically assail the defensive
positions surrounding the village, and make an
end of the matter. Meanwhile it seems clear
that the whole of the Turkish Army of Widdin,
under Osman Pasha, are in and about Plevna—
nearly thirty thousand men! "Why, we had
never given Widdin a thought—knew nothing
of any such army as that—and here they all are
suddenly massed on our right flank, as though
they had dropped down from the clouds. Well,
they must be smashed!"

Alas! what scene is this, as darkness descends
on the evening of the 31st July? A bugler is
sounding the assembly at the Prince's order, and
a few stragglers of several regiments gather to
the sound; presently a detachment comes up,
sullen and silent, out of the Plevna valley; it is
barely a company; then a squadron of dragoons.
Are these all that come to the General's call?
All! Where is the Russian army? Down
there in the hollows between the ridges, dead by
thousands, wounded by thousands; the surviving
remnants still fighting, here and there, as the

moon rises; all over the vast battlefield the victorious Turks firing fiercely into broken groups, and driving them away. And what other sounds are these which assail the ear of the Prince as he stands on the ridge, with the meagre escort which his bugle-call has gathered out of the wreck? Dark forms are moving over the corpse-strewn ground; up out of the valley come moans, shrieks for mercy, yells of barbarous triumph. The throats of thousands of helpless men are being cut by the accursed fiends. The horror, the agony, the despair of that night! Defeat and disaster have overtaken the Russian arms, and as the shattered remnants of a splendid army trickle into Sistova, the question for the Czar is not " When shall we cross the mountains?" but " Shall we be driven into the river?"

What, then, is to be done? Shall the troops be withdrawn from Tirnova and the Schipka Pass, and from the line of the Lom where the Czarevitch faces eastward, defending the left flank; shall they with one mighty effort pluck

out this thorn planted in the right flank, over-
whelm Osman, blot out Plevna and its trenches
from the map of Bulgaria? The Czar says "No";
the Bulgarian peasants cannot be abandoned to
the mercy of the Turk; the troops must stand,
where they are, on the defensive until reinforcements move up. The ukase goes forth, mobilizing
the Guards, the Grenadiers, and two divisions—
120,000 men in all, with 460 guns, for duty at
the front, and 220,000 to replace losses and stand
in reserve. Holy Russia will gladly send forth
the men. The Prince of Roumania is also
appealed to; he replies with 37,000 men and
84 guns.

Now, once more, a great opportunity for the
Turk! If, now, the Sultan would bring along
that Sacred Banner, and his apparently still more
sacred person, raise the former and display the
latter, what could he not do? An advance in
force from Rustchuk or Rasgrad would compel
the Russian armies—dispirited by the disaster at
Plevna—to mass for a decisive battle. Osman,
also, could sally forth, and the chances would be

that the Christian host would be ground to death between two millstones long before the reinforcements came. Instead of all this, Suleiman and his army bang their heads against the Schipka Pass and get hard knocks. Close to them is a pass through which they might advance without losing a man, and join hands with Mehemet Ali. But poor Mehemet is a foreigner and no Turk, and Suleiman won't have anything to do with him. The Sublime Porte approves of Suleiman's suicidal operations in the Schipka Pass, and Mehemet Ali is left to make his effort alone. He makes it, and it fizzles out. So the month of August is allowed to pass—the golden opportunity is lost. Religion and jealousy combine to destroy the Turkish Empire.

But Osman, the greatest soldier of all the crowd of generals and pashas in Bulgaria, he who has twice sent the Russians reeling down the Plevna slopes, how does he employ himself during the month of deadlock? By the 1st September he has eighteen redoubts ready, manned and armed. The three principal ones two at Grivitza on the east, and one at Krishin on the south, command the whole country around Plevna. Besides these there are long lines of trenches and batteries, all so contrived as to unite and support the earthworks. Osman has created a great fortress, so great, so dangerous that the whole power of Russia *must* be concentrated against it, *must* attack it, *must* take it, before a single step can be made in the direction of Constantinople. So now, in the first week of September, the curtain once more rises for the third act of this ghastly drama of Plevna.

Twenty heavy Russian siege guns have come up, and are in position; more than two hundred field pieces stand pointed at the redoubts. On the 7th September, at six in the morning, the first shot of the new attack is fired. All that day, and the three following days, the artillery on both sides roars from morning till night. The fire of 100 guns is concentrated on the Grivitza redoubt, and, after two days of it, the eight guns in the redoubt have been pounded into silence. On the 11th there are 250 guns in position against the works, and a still more terrific cannonade is maintained. The earth and air tremble with the din, the face of heaven is obscured by the smoke.

The Czar, the Grand Duke Nicholas, and the Prince of Roumania are present. It is the name-day of the Emperor, and the assault is ordered for three o'clock.

Once more the same terrible scenes that were witnessed on July 30th are witnessed again. Regiment after regiment is sent down into the valley to the attack of the redoubts. Once more they are met with a withering rifle fire which mows them down. The survivors, with more than mortal daring, press on up the glacis, are unsupported, and, after clinging to the very parapets, are sent reeling back. Skobeleff and his men actually carry the redoubt which they attack, and hold it, at a cost of 3,000 men. Five times the Turks try to drive them out; five times they are beaten back; the sixth time they succeed, and the worn-out men, unassisted by reinforcements, are forced to fly, all save one

heroic band, which, refusing to leave the redoubt,
perishes there to the last man.

Skobeleff, covered with mud, his sword broken,
his white Arab horse killed, his face black with
smoke, his eyes bloodshot, mad with the fury of
battle, rages at his defeat. In the evening in his
tent he is calm and collected as though there
were no battlefield within a thousand miles of
him. "I have done my best," he says, "I could
do no more. My detachment is half destroyed;
my regiments do not exist; I have no officers
left; they sent me no reinforcements, I have
lost three guns. But I blame nobody; it is the
will of God." Kriloff, too, has failed. His
gallant fellows rushed into the jaws of destruction;
flaming volleys sent them staggering back down
the glacis, which is strewn with thousands of
their dead and wounded. The survivors sullenly
come up out of the valley of death. But what is
that yonder, over the Grivitza redoubt? The
Roumanian flag! Then the famous redoubt has
fallen! It fell at sundown to the third assault,
and the banner of Prince Charles waves over

SKOBELEFF.

heaps of dead and dying which completely fill the interior. It is not manned and held by the victors ; it cannot be, for not three hundred yards away there is another redoubt, from which the Turks command it. A barren success, which counts for little as against the terrible disasters of the day.

Three hundred and fifty officers, seventeen thousand men lie on those bloody slopes, dead and wounded together. Again that horror! Dark forms move about; once more merciless fiends glut themselves with gore ; once more, as the sun goes down, men shudder as cries for mercy ascend out of the dark valley, cries cut short by the knife of the assassin—

"Spare me, for Christ's sake!"——

"Die, dog, in the name of the Prophet!"

If it takes every man in Russia this accursed fortress shall fall!

The Czar orders a winter campaign, and sends for the Defender of Sebastopol.

Todleben shall take Plevna.

# CHAPTER VIII.

## Todleben Triumphant.

TODLEBEN, of Sebastopol, shall take Plevna! That, after three crushing defeats, was the decision of the Czar. Todleben, who held the English and French at bay twenty-three years ago, shall see what he can do, now that Osman, the Turk, stands at bay in this earth-built Bulgarian fortress. No splendid harbour, or dockyards, or arsenal, or great forts of masonry here; only a little town lying in the downs, girt about with trenches and redoubts. But *such* trenches and redoubts! Constructed, as these are, by as great a master of defence as Todleben himself, Sebastopol, with its Malakoff and Redan, its land forts and sea forts, was not more scientifically guarded than this hitherto unknown Bulgarian town. Osman

TODLEBEN, OF SEBASTOPOL.

H

defends, Todleben attacks—it is a contest of giants, and the world stands at gaze.

The failure of the great assault of the 11th September leaves the Russians paralysed; they withdraw to the positions they held during the four days' cannonade which preceded the attack, and they are in no mood to renew the attempt, even though Todleben and the Imperial Guard do come to help.  The terrible fate of the wounded weighs upon the soldier's mind; he knows, now, that a wound received during an attack means assassination; where he falls there will he be butchered.  His courage is not proof against so hideous a prospect.  Plevna must be regularly besieged by the great engineer, and a winter campaign must be faced.  It *is* faced with all the determination which belongs to a death struggle.  Here, then, on Plevna heights it shall be fought out to the bitter end.  The Roumanians, from the captured Grivitza redoubt, attack the other redoubt which commands it. Hot work at 250 yards! but the attack fails, and now there is nothing for it but to pit spade

against spade, and work up to the redoubt by
flying sap.

Meanwhile Kriloff is told off to command the
cavalry, to get in the rear of Plevna, and cut
off supplies coming from Sofia. Kriloff cannot
do it; a large Turkish force of all arms brings
in a convoy of 2,000 wagons under his very
nose. He guards the Sofia road, as he is told
to do, but, behold! another convoy gets past him
by taking a parallel road, which he knew nothing
about, and loses only two oxen! The only news
of comfort comes from Schipka. Suleiman is
still battering away at the Pass, but Radetzky
stands firm; he holds the gate through which
the army will march upon Constantinople. But
when? Many a weary week hence; not until
the mountains are covered with snow.

And in Constantinople itself, are the people
jubilant? Does the Porte, exulting in Osman's
victories, strike the stars with Sublime head?
This unpleasant fact stares Porte and Sultan in
the face: that when news comes of a Turkish
victory Turkish "consolidés" fall; when a defeat

is announced they rise. Bitter fact! But
Osman knows little of "consolidés," and cares
less. What he does know is that Todleben and
the Russian Guard have arrived; that a smarter
man than Kriloff is on the Sofia road, and that
no more convoys get through. Gourko has
closed the road.

It is the middle of October, and the invest-
ment of Plevna is complete. Osman is shut
up; he must fight his way out or surrender.
And what is Todleben doing? One thing he is
*not* doing; he is not attempting to capture by
direct assault strongly entrenched positions held
by determined men with breech-loaders and
bristling with Krupp guns. That folly he will
not commit. But he is bombarding on a strange
and gigantic scale. Two or three times a day a
terrific crash rends the sky; three hundred guns,
massed and concentrated upon one spot are
simultaneously fired, now at the earthworks, now
at the town; sometimes, but seldom, at men.
For Osman's men are not caught so easily; they
have burrowed out of sight.

November comes; and now there are 120,000 men round the doomed town. Osman is ringed in with iron, and is eating himself up. But what a man he is! Deserters bring word that he is already on short commons, and yet there on the hills the Russians observe a herd of many thousand cattle which had not been seen before. Plenty of beef still! Beef and bread now are Osman's best weapons; shot and shell have done their work. And so the great question all through November was: "Will Osman, when his provisions are gone, surrender, or try to cut his way out?" Everywhere throughout the besieging host the hope was fervently cherished that he would adopt the latter course and come out and fight. Then could be exacted the penalty for the fiendish brutalities his men have committed; then the thousands of slaughtered wounded could be avenged. "Let the wild beasts come out of their den, and be shot down in fair fight." Such was the hope of the Russians, from Grand Duke to drummer.

There they sit, then, all through November,

these two armies, looking at each other. The Russians, who had not hesitated to attack in September with 60,000 men, do not now dare to do so with twice that force; and the Turks, not so strong as they were then, are as ready as ever to defend their earthworks. As for breaking out, that hope has gone, for the Russian and Roumanian entrenchments round Plevna are now quite as strong as the defensive works; in the weakest part of their line the Russians can mass the fire of sixty guns. Evidently Osman is in bad case.

December now; and the first fall of snow whitens the ground, and hides the ghastly tokens of the months of fighting since July. The bones of many thousands of gallant fellows, which lay festering and rotting beneath the summer sun, are out of sight now under the soft, white covering, and their living comrades hail the familiar spectacle of a snow-clad landscape. The siege is conducted in a happy-go-lucky, leisurely sort of fashion, and there seems to be a tacit understanding that there shall be no more severe fighting. Osman holds out, content to detain a vast army on this side of the Balkans. The Grand Duke is satisfied with blockading the troublesome fortress, and is prepared to sit there before it until it is starved into submission. But it becomes more and more evident that the end is at hand; spies come out from the town, and report that bread is scarce; and though meat is plentiful, there is no wood for cooking it. All hope of relief from Sofia or from Suleiman's army is abandoned; the Czarewitch's line, which holds back the only other Turkish army on this side the Balkans, has been attacked time and again since August, but, though bent, has never been broken; Gourko has gone raiding again over the mountains, and keeps the Sofia road; Radetzky guards Schipka. Surely Plevna totters to its fall!

December 10th: A dull, snowy night, but the Russian troops are in good spirits, and the lines are thronged with soldiers cooking their dinners and singing a welcome to the familiar weather, such an improvement as it is on the torrents of

rain and seas of mud which ushered in the
Bulgarian winter. But why, in Skobeleff's section
of the siege-works, is there such unwonted stir?
A spy has come out of the town with the news
that Osman has issued three days' rations, and a
new pair of sandals to each man. Another spy
arrives soon after; his story is that the garrison
of Plevna is concentrating near the bridge over
the river, at the back of the town. Before the
night is gone a third spy announces that the Turks
have abandoned their redoubts and trenches.
Skobeloff, throwing forward a portion of his force
in the dim light, finds that it is so; the terrible
Krishine forts are deserted, and the Russians
have only to walk in. The morning breaks at
last, and then it is seen that the whole line of
defences—those terrible defences which have
defied the might of Russia for four months—are
abandoned. The telegraph which encircles the
whole line of siege-works flashes the news around,
and the whole host of the besiegers are on the
alert. The supreme moment has arrived! The
spies are right; Osman is about to attempt to

break through the toils! Scarcely have the first
streaks of dawn broken the grey Eastern sky,
and lighted up the snow-covered ridges and
valleys, when a sudden burst of cannon shots,
instantly followed by the rattling crash of infantry
fire, announces that the final conflict has begun.
Away at the back of the town dense clouds of
smoke show that it is there that Osman seeks his
outlet; and certainly it is not there that he will
find it, for the Russian Guard has been massed
for weeks at that point, in expectation of the
sortie which has now commenced.

Grand and terrible is the catastrophe of the
great tragedy of Plevna, and quite in keeping
with the terrific scenes that have preceded it.
The manner in which Osman is making his
attempt is remarkable. The first thing seen by
the Russian force, against which the attack is
directed, is a long line of bullock-waggons issuing
from the town. Behind their cover is the
Turkish army. Instantly the fire of 100 guns,
and volleys from thousands of Berdan rifles are
concentrated upon the baggage train. A hail of

OSMAN, OF PLEVNA.

shells and bullets smashes the waggons, and kills the cattle and their drivers by scores. The maddened animals stream over the plain; and now the sortie is fully developed. The Turkish infantry, deprived of its cover, makes a fierce dash straight at the line of trenches held by the Sibrersky regiment, sweeps into them like a whirlwind, captures a battery of artillery, and, in fierce hand-to-hand fight, bayonets the defenders where they stand. So the Turk *can* capture entrenchments as well as he can defend them! This brilliant and daring assault proves it. But it is a useless feat of arms; the strength of the Russian lines is such that no attack can succeed. While the victorious Turks are in the captured battery the Grenadier Brigade is brought up by Strukoff and hurled against them. Once more a desperate struggle rages round the cannon; in a few minutes the Turks are sent reeling back to the broken waggons, and from there still further back to the deep banks of the river. There they reform and open fire.

The sortie is repulsed, and the fate of Osman

is decided, for the defences of Plevna, now in his rear, are in the hands of the Russians. Until mid-day the cannonade is maintained ; then it ceases ; the fire of the breechloaders dies away ; the smoke lifts ; silence reigns—a silence not again to be broken by sounds of war.

Now, see! a Turkish officer rides out over the bridge with a white flag, and a shout of joy arises from the Russian host. The siege of Plevna is over. Osman has surrendered. The hero himself lies wounded in a little house near the bridge, but later he comes out in a carriage, escorted by Cossacks, and followed by his own officers. The Grand Duke Nicholas rides up, and he and Osman look at each other for a few moments without speaking. Then the Grand Duke holds out his hand. Osman takes it. "I compliment you on your defence of Plevna," says Nicholas, "it is one of the most splendid military feats in history." Osman smiles, rises, bows, then reseats himself. "Osman Ghazi he is," says young Skobeloff, "and Osman the Victorious he will remain, in spite of his surrender."

Passing over the plain, ploughed and torn by shell and bullet, strewn with dead and dying men and horses and oxen, littered with the shattered fragments of the baggage train, Osman the Victorious, greeted as he goes by the chivalrous and respectful salutes of his enemies, leaves the little town which his genius has made one of the historic spots of the world.

# CHAPTER IX.

## 𝔅ugbears of 𝔅ulgaria.

"THE inscription on the banners of Russia is 'Emancipation of the Christians of the East!'" So said Prince Charles of Roumania, in his proclamation to his people after his declaration of war against the common enemy—"and the inscription on the banner of Roumania is 'Independence.'" How thoroughly each country has acted up to its motto, the actual condition of Roumania and Bulgaria proves. He who was Prince in 1877 is now King, and a telegram in the daily papers is full of significance: "The forts around Bucharest are now nearly ready, and, when completed, will form the strongest entrenched position in Europe." Roumania, then, has laid to heart the lesson taught by Osman the Victorious, and Bucharest is stronger

than Plevna—a very decided step towards independence! Little did Czar Alexander and astute
Ignatieff realize what would be the upshot of that
clause, then so glorious-sounding, of the Treaty of
San Stefano, made within sight of the dome
of St. Sophia : "Bulgaria is constituted an autonomous, tributary Principality, with a Christian
Government and a national militia." For that
clause tens of thousands of men laid down their
lives on the fatal glacis of the Plevna forts, in
many a fight on the Lom, in the frozen passes
of the Balkans, in pitched battles on the plain
of Philippopolis ; for that clause the Czar of all
the Russias was content to direct the affairs of a
mighty empire from headquarters in a Bulgarian
hut ; in grateful anticipation of that clause the
Bulgarian peasants kissed the stirrups and the
clothes of their liberators, strewed their way with
flowers, knelt before them as though the Host
was being borne through their land. And now ?
Well, now there is that "strongest entrenched
position in Europe" on one side of the river, and
a very decidedly "autonomous" principality, with

I

an extremely pugnacious "militia," on the other.
The history of 1877 cannot repeat itself in 1894.
To a Russian, the story of the war for the
emancipation of Bulgaria must read very much
like that fable of Æsop, which tells of the
countryman who nursed the numbed viper in
his bosom and warmed it by his fireside; with
this difference, that the mattock of the Czar
cannot be wielded as was that of the countryman.
The ungrateful Bulgarian viper cannot be struck
dead!

And to us, who saw the Emancipation accom-
plished in that terrible summer and winter, how
strange it all seems! Autonomy and a militia!
Take this little scene:—Two correspondents,
weary of the monotony of life at Rustchuk, in
the early days of the war, ere yet a Russian had
set foot in Bulgaria, are taking a little ride along
the road outside the town. They come to the
village of Dolabkoi. It lies in the valley of the
Lom; the pretty houses of its thrifty inhabitants
are set snugly in the midst of garden-like orchards
and fields, past which the little stream flows soft

and clear—a perfect Arcadia. Charmed at the sight of it, the correspondents ride into the village. Their appearance is the signal for confusion; doors are hastily shut, children cry, women run, dogs bark. Dolabkoi is panic-struck. Why? Behind one of the correspondents ride his two servants, *Circassians*. It is the servants and not the masters who have struck terror into the population; the dreaded Tcherkess are upon them, mortal foes who hate and despise the Bulgar race; freebooters, who rob and maltreat whenever they can find an opportunity; men so terrible that the Bulgarian peasant counts himself lucky if his women escape unmolested from their vicinity. The correspondents ride on and stop at the little wine shop. The moment they catch sight of the Tcherkess, the villagers there retire to one side of the room and sit silent, cowering. The host will not take a single piastre for the wine consumed; he *dares* not under the eye of the "bandit."

The two Tcherkess smile complacently, and offer to procure for their master (without payment) anything he may require in the village—anything. The offer is sternly declined, and the invaders who have so seriously upset the equanimity of Dolabkoi depart. To their employer these Tcherkess are faithful servants, ready, willing, obedient—as mild-mannered men as ever cut a throat. To the Bulgar, whose throat is in question, they are fiends to flee from, to tremble before. A significant little scene, this, in the happy valley of the Lom, which seems to make that clause of the treaty quite desirable, for he is quite a familiar sight in the Bulgaria of 1877, this Circassian horseman, in his long coat, with a row of cartridges across the breast, and his fur cap; a dagger in its handsome sheath of niello is at his waist, and a gun in a curious hairy case slung across his back. Evidently he is as perfectly able, as he is undoubtedly ready, to "clean out" a Bulgarian village, single-handed.

A much more picturesque object than the Tcherkess is another of the bugbears of Bulgaria —the Zeibeck. He hails from the neighbourhood of Smyrna, and the Sublime Porte has imported him, thinking to make an irregular soldier of him, and to strike terror into the Russians with him. Unfortunately he terrifies the Sublime Porte itself, and is shipped back again as soon as possible, but not before giving us a taste of his quality in Constantinople and in Bulgaria.

Never to be forgotten is the Zeibeck! Behold him as he walks the streets of Pera in the intervals between his drillings in the camp. He is brown and muscular, and he swaggers along, carrying with unconscious grace the most astonishing costume worn on earth by mortal man. Round his head a turban is wrapped, and piled up to the height of a foot or more; it is surmounted by a dome-like cap, padded to keep its shape; a long fringe hangs down from it about his ears. A silk shirt, open in front, beneath a very short gold-embroidered jacket; round his waist an immense sash, stuffed with strange weapons and hung with pouches. Short breeches, ending above the knee, cloth greaves, and leather shoes complete the lower man.  The whole of the costume is of bright colours, but the embroidery of his jacket and the glitter of his weapons seem to harmonise the crudeness of the tints, and give the Zeibeck an *ensemble* which is not to be matched for barbaric picturesqueness.  In his own country he is said to be hospitable and inoffensive ; transplanted to European Turkey he became a bugbear of the first order.  The Bulgarians, already trembling beneath the scowl of the Turk and the Tcherkess, viewed his importation with dismay.  To us western strangers the Zeibeck was a travelling curiosity-shop ; we gazed with wonder at his piled-up head-gear ; at his swords, long and short, straight and curved ; at his sheaths of embossed silver, his flint-lock pistols with handles of ivory and damascened locks and barrels.  But to the Bulgar this arsenal of weapons simply suggested the death of a dozen Christians by distinct and separate methods.  As it was quite certain that the Zeibeck made no distinction between Russian and Bulgarian, but was equally ready to go for either on sight, he was at once placed on the same favoured footing as the Tcherkess—on the free list!

I travelled from Varna to Shumla in the same train with the regiment of Zeibecks who had been hurriedly sent off to the front by the authorities, and at one of the stations, where a halt was made for dinner, two of the biggest and brownest of the barbarians treated us to a dance. A ring was formed and a motley crowd gathered to see the performance. One of the Zeibecks seated himself, cross-legged, and, unslinging from his back a small, guitar-like instrument, twanged upon it a curious measure, very monotonous but well accented. His companion immediately began figuring with his legs, pointing his toes and planting his heels, and now and again snapping his fingers. Then, raising one leg and extending it horizontally, he slowly pirouetted on the other in a manner highly ludicrous to western eyes, but regarded with the utmost solemnity by his companions. Having completed this *pas seul* at one side of the ring, the dancer suddenly uttered a yell and rushed to the other end. The crowd fell back before him, but he suddenly stopped and resumed the pirouette. Then he unsheathed two of his swords and began a sort of sword play, which ended in his placing them with their naked points in his girdle and hopping about as though slowly expiring from mortal wounds. Out came the swords again, and, with another yell, he whirled them about and rushed across the ring, scattering the sand and gravel. The spectators broke and fled. When they rallied, there was the Zeibeck, solemnly turning on one leg, without a trace of excitement on his features—a strange scene, upon which the shrill whistle of the engine broke with startling incongruity!

The question with us was how these irregular troops of the Turkish Army could ever be kept in hand and prevented from breaking loose to pillage and massacre at will. The question was answered for us, at the very next station, by another strange and truly Oriental scene. It so happened that no less a person than the new Governor, or Vali, of Rustchuk, was on the train

by which we were travelling. At the last station
before entering the town the Governor was
asked to pronounce judgment in a dispute
between a Turk and Bulgar. It appears that

TWO DOZEN AND A HALF.

a mixed gang of Turkish irregulars and Bulgars
were engaged in repairing part of the line, when
one of the Bulgars, having offended a Turk, the
latter flung a hammer at his opponent's head,
inflicting a severe wound. The Turk was

brought to the station under arrest, and the case was laid before the Vali, who, after hearing both sides of the story, ordered the prisoner to receive thirty strokes. In a moment the man's head was in "chancery," and a heavy stick descended thirty times upon that portion of the person which is provided by Nature for the reception of castigation. Had the back been a Bulgarian one the stick could not have been wielded with a better will. Execution done, the train moved on, and we were soon in the midst of sterner scenes; but the Zeibeck dance and the Vali's judgment came as welcome comic interludes in the grim drama of war.

# CHAPTER X.

## The Old Turk and the New.

JULES DETROIT is a queer name for
a Turkish General; but it so happened
that the man once known as Jules Detroit,
French by descent, German by education, Turk
by choice, famous in 1877 as Mehemet Ali
Pasha, was the instrument chosen by fate to
give to His Majesty, the present Czar of All
the Russias, an extremely unpleasant quarter of
an hour. Poor Mehemet Ali! in his little hour
the pride and hope of the Turkish Empire in
Europe, but destined to early disgrace and
assassination. Those who witnessed his desperate attempt to save his adopted country have not
yet forgotten his kindness and courtesy, at a time
when months of brutality and insult had made
the burden of "special correspondent with the

Turkish Army" almost too heavy to bear; they
remember with sympathy his bitter saying: "I
have been dismissed because I refused to break
my neck against a stone wall." Of all the
Generals, Russian or Turkish, whose reputations
were wrecked by the great war, this Franco-
German renegade was the one most entitled to
sympathy. His brief career in Bulgaria afforded
a remarkable instance of the inherent rottenness
of the state of Turkey.

Here is a picture of the Turkish Army of the
Quadrilateral in that summer of 1877—an army,
it must be remembered, whose rank and file was
of the finest possible fighting material, fully
equal to the best that Russia could show. At
the head of it is the "old Turk," Abdul Kerim,
once schoolfellow of Von Moltke. Like Von
Moltke he is a man of plans, the great difference
between the two strategists being that Abdul
Kerim's plans are simply stupid. Behold him
——seated in his splendid tent, his "plan" in his
head, a knowing smile on his fat old face, as he
assures his European visitors that the crossing

of the river by the Russians and their advance
to the Balkans occasion him no perturbation.
Nothing but the announcement that dinner was
not quite ready ever did disturb the mind of
Abdul. Shumla, the impregnable fortress, was
to be held by the main body of the Turkish
forces, and, when the time came, Abdul would
sally forth and destroy the Muscovite host.
Alas! poor Abdul! Your old schoolfellow could
have told you what would happen—what *did*
happen. The first care of the Russians was to
stretch a cordon of troops from river to mountains and *mask* the fortress of Rustchuk and
Shumla. Had Abdul remained in charge of his
army he would have seen his enemies, whom he
had planned to destroy, march past his favourite
fortress and go on their way, leaving him and his
plan blockaded. Abdul was spared this; but a
worse thing happened to him. To his camp at
Shumla came Namyk Pasha and Redif Pasha.
Old Namyk was a secret councillor of the
Sultan, Redif was Minister of War; both came
from Constantinople, from the very presence of

the Sultan. Their mission was, apparently, to
stir up Abdul and make him do something, but
in reality Redif was told to watch Abdul, to try
and ascertain what his "plan" was; whether to
resist the Russian invasion, or to sell his country
to the invader. Namyk's instructions were still
more interesting. He was to watch both Abdul
and Redif. This intrigue, so thoroughly Turkish
in its triangularity, soon arrived at its crisis.
Like a thunderbolt the news ran round the
army that the old Sirdar was deposed, that his
successor, Mehemet Ali, was even now in Bulgaria, and was hourly awaited at Shumla. Sure
enough Mehemet Ali arrived, assumed command,
made a fine speech, and positively brought new
life and new hope to the army, which, under the
spell of Abdul's "plan," was becoming rapidly
demoralised. No sooner had Mehemet Ali
appeared than it became known, that not only
was Abdul deposed but that Redif was also in
disgrace. Namyk had evidently watched them
both to some purpose! Orders go forth that
they are to leave Shumla at once, and go to

Constantinople. Abdul, as usual, is hungry, and wants some dinner before starting. "Are they gone?" says Namyk. "They are dining," is the reply. "Is it thus that the Sultan's commands are fulfilled?" roars the old man; "let them be off." Then comes a scene which we behold with pity and wonder. Hustled from the table, old Abdul gets into a common country cart, and un-attended, almost unnoticed, drives away into the darkness.

He, who a few hours ago was the supreme head of the Turkish armies in the field, whose slightest wish was law, had come to this. The very servants who had stood trembling in his presence did not dare even to recognise him.

The new Commander-in-Chief soon showed himself to be a man of energy. His spirit ran through the army like wildfire; the Army of the Quadrilateral was to be up and doing at last. And to us poor "specials," bullied as we had been week after week, what a God-send he was, this Franco-German Turk, with a pupil of Saint Cyr as his Chief-of-Staff! Here were men who actually looked at newspapers, and did not see a spy in every European. Our joy was somewhat dashed by the news that the Marshal, Achmet Eyoub, our bugbear, who always treated us with insolent suspicion, was to remain. That Mehemet disliked him was clear; it was also evident that Achmet was too strong at Constantinople to be disturbed in Bulgaria. But the Marshal was not quite so free with his insults now, and could hunt for spies in the quarter where he would be most likely to find them—in the Bulgarian quarter of every town and village in the country. The mental and bodily condition of the Bulgars was an unfailing source of wonder and amusement to us. Everywhere they were in a state of suppressed agitation. Insurgents at heart, but fearing for life and property, they followed the progress of the war with astonishing quickness and intelligence, and were always well-informed as to military movements. The Russians, whether at Plevna, or on the Lom, could always count upon information from the enemy's camp. This being well known to the Turks, the astonishing thing to us was, not that here and there some Bulgarian was maltreated, or some village plundered by Bashi-Bazouks, but that there were not wholesale massacres.   Did we ride into some Bulgar village, the inhabitants would anxiously inquire into our political opinions.   If they were friendly, they would forthwith pour out a torrent of abuse upon the Turks ; if the strangers' views were anti-Russian, the villager's mouth (and door) were kept tightly shut.   That we felt, one and all, a sort of pitying contempt for the Bulgar is certain.   We saw in 1877 no indications that the dawn of liberty would brighten so quickly into promising sunshine, and we were considerably puzzled by the fact that evidences of Turkish oppression and tyranny were difficult to discover, in the midst of the material prosperity which the Bulgarians enjoyed.   Even under the heavy tax upon their industry exacted by the Porte, they thrived upon their fertile fields, and, for all we could see, were better off than the Turkish population.   The Russian liberator himself was somewhat taken aback when he came into actual

K

contact with the Bulgar, whom he came to set
free. "We have been labouring under a mis-
conception as to the condition of the Bulgarian
Christians. We believed them to be oppressed,
impoverished, impeded in the exercise of their
religion, not sure of their lives for an hour, not
sure of the honour of their women, or of their
property. And so we were thrilled with enthusiasm for a veritable war of liberation. But how
do we actually find the Bulgar? He lives in
perfect comfort; our own peasant cannot be
compared with him in comfort, competence, or
prosperity." Thus did Russian officers express
themselves to the correspondents with their
army, and the correspondents added their own
testimony. "I should be glad," wrote one of
them, "if the English peasantry were as well off.
The grain crops of the Bulgarian stretch far
and wide. Every village has its herds; last
year's straw is yet in the stack-yards; milk may
be bought in every house. And while the Bulgar
is awaiting his liberation—objecting strongly to
the decided chance of having his throat cut

A Bulgarian Atrocity.

pending its achievement—he has as excellent a notion of turning an honest penny as any Yankee or Scot, and 'sticks' the Russian unmercifully. The liberators pay for all Bulgarian property they consume in the way of forage and provisions. And they have to pay! The Bulgar realises that in this matter he is a master of the situation, and he puts money in his purse."

While he is quietly lining his pockets, four great armies are afield, two in a grapple for life or death at Plevna, two standing face to face along the Lom Valley, watching for an opportunity to come to blows. Not till the advent of Mehemet Ali did this opportunity arrive; but in the middle of July the swift downfall of Abdul prepared the way, and we were soon to witness a phase of the campaign, which, though by no means comparable to the struggle at Plevna, was of great interest as a military operation.

I have followed out in these War Notes the main features of the war down to the capture of Osman's stronghold, and now, going back to the time when the invaders received their first check

there, I propose to tell the story of Mehemet
Ali's attempt to break through the army of the
Czarewitch, which stood between him and his
beleagured comrade.    Success in the attempt
meant annihilation for the Russians; failure
meant the dismemberment of Turkey.

The destiny of the Ottoman Empire seemed
to be in the hands of the Franco-German, Jules
Detroit.

# CHAPTER XI.

## Skirmish and Massacre.

HAVING got rid of the Commander-in-Chief, the "old Turk" Abdul, the new Commander, Mehemet Ali, found himself in possession of a fine army, with a fine opportunity for using it, and before July was out he had already put an edge on the tremendous weapon which time and fate had placed in his hands. He was going to deal a swashing blow at the Czarewitch—that was certain; the Russian army, which stood between Mehemet and his colleague Osman, and which had dared to push cavalry reconnaissances within sight of the great fortresses of the quadrilateral, Rustchuk and Shumla, must first be pushed back, then broken through, so that the two Turkish commanders might join forces, drive the beaten enemy into the river, and so bring to an end the Czar's crusade.

Here was the opportunity, created by Osman and the stubborn earth-works of Plevna; and here, apparently, was the man, Mehemet Ali, formerly Jules Detroit. Osman was to stand firm in the west, while Mehemet, incessantly moving, was to hew a way to him from the east. Between the two the Russians, facing both ways, would have to fight for dear life. Such was the opportunity—such the plan. Mehemet Ali's European brain was quick enough to recognise the one and conceive the other, and the audacity of the Czarewitch's cavalry kept his wits sharp. For Archduke Vladimir's Cossacks had passed the River Lom, ridden right across the Turkish line of communications, and actually cut the railway and telegraph between Rustchuk and Rasgrad. Scouting in pairs, the raiders had struck the line, blown away thirty feet of it with dynamite, climbed the telegraph-posts and broken the wires, and then had remounted and galloped back, without the loss of a man, before

A Raid on the Wires.

the Turks had time to rub their eyes and realise that such a raid was possible.

Thus, at last, after being pounded with siege artillery from the opposite side of the river, Rustchuk was now isolated on the land side. We had seen the last train steam away, laden with Turkish families, mostly women—a weird crowd of silent, veiled figures, like sheeted spectres on their way to another world, an English engine-driver their Charon, and the train his barge. They glided off into the darkness, and, when we returned to the deserted town, we felt that the Rustchuk-Varna Railway had played its part in the war, and that henceforth we must trust to our horses. The cutting of the railway brought the fact of war home to us more than the roar of batteries and the crash of shells. Nothing brings one's powers of self-reliance into play quicker than the fact that the enemy is on the line of communication.

Bilderling's dragoons, too, had been raiding up and down the Lom and across it, and had come into contact with the Circassians and Bashi-

Bazouks. From Kaceljevo, a village on the debateable land between the armies, came a terrible story. Bilderling's regiment, which had its quarters there, rode out one day on a reconnaissance, leaving about a hundred Bulgarian villagers in their homes. While the Russians were away, a detachment of Turks swooped down upon the little place. The villagers fled in terror into the church, but there was no sanctuary for them at a Christian altar from such an enemy. The door was broken in, and not a soul was spared. When the dragoons came back they found Kaceljevo empty, and the church a shambles. Presently, some terrified wretches who had hidden in the gardens crept out and told the colonel what had happened. The reeking church told its own story.

It was not this bloody deed alone which taught the army of the Czarewitch what kind of an enemy it had to deal with. Already several of the bodies of the troopers killed in outpost skirmishes had been found decapitated and otherwise mutilated, and it had become a point of honour with the Russians to remove from the field, not their wounded only, but their dead. And so, after a skirmish on the Lom, the strange and terrible spectacle was seen of retiring troops, accompanied by long strings of riderless horses—riderless, but each with a corpse across its back, the arms and head of the body swinging on one side, the legs on the other, the blood of the death-wound streaming downwards to the earth and leaving a ghastly trail. The Valkyrie myth of the Scandinavians came rushing into one's mind at the sight, and the fancy which pictured the War-maidens riding, with clang of thunder and flash of lightning, athwart the sky, each bearing a dead warrior to Walhalla, found reflection, here, among these death-freighted horses.

As in the west, at Plevna, so here on the Lom, the Russian troops, burning with indignation, vowed vengeance and no quarter. In the east, as in the west, it was war to the knife, and the Russian roll-call after battle had little need to account for " wounded and missing " ; those who

had not returned alive were dead—and there an
end.

Of the fantastic brutalities of the Turks,
especially of the irregular troops, the Tcherkess
and the Bashi-Bazouks, which swarmed round
the regular army, there were many witnesses.
Consuls, correspondents, military attachés—all
saw with their eyes and heard with their ears
things which would otherwise have been in-
credible.    Whether the consuls and attachés
reported them to their foreign offices and war
offices at home I know not, but it is quite certain
that the correspondents with the Turkish armies
in  Bulgaria  did  not  report  them  to  their
newspapers.    Why?    The  war  correspondent
was *muzzled* by the Political Commission, the
Board  of  Censors,  which  accompanied  headquarters,  and  without  whose  countersign  no
telegram  could  be  sent.    When  a  telegraphic
message,  cut  down  into  a  mere  bald  scrap
of "news" did finally get to Constantinople,
it  was  sat  upon  by  another  board,  which
squeezed  a  little  more  life  out  of  it.    The

papers of Constantinople were also gagged by
decree : " By order of the Minister of War, the
local journals are forbidden to publish any matter
relating to the war, or incidents of battles, or any
collateral facts bearing on the subject." Most
concise and complete! And the penalty for
disobedience was suppression, or expulsion, or
both. " Special telegrams from our Correspondent with the Turkish Army " were, therefore,
few, feeble, and far between, and the only course
left open to a correspondent was to send letters
through the post. Here, again, though much
more could be done than by wire, we were beset
by three difficulties ; the post itself was not safe ;
our journals came back with our letters in them,
and were carefully overhauled by the Porte ; and,
finally, sometimes there was no post at all.
Evidence that letters were actually opened was
not directly forthcoming, but it was explained to
us by one well versed in Turkish mysteries, how
a carefully sealed letter could be opened, read,
resealed, and sent on. So it happened that the
British public was not kept informed of several

"incidents of battles" and "collateral facts" which would have startled them, and dispelled any remaining tendency to disbelieve the horror of Batak. The disclosure of that bloody piece of work, made by a correspondent—fearless Macgahan—before the war, had gone far to convince the upper classes in England that the Turk was not quite such a " gentleman " as they thought; but we, who followed the Turkish armies, were not able to bring forward our evidence that, in point of fact, he was not a gentleman at all.

On the other hand, we were "invited"—very firmly invited—to describe in full a certain remarkable incident, which came to our notice, and which duly appeared in the newspapers, under the head of " Cossack Cruelties." Most hideous cruelties they were, and as we had ocular evidence of them, and as the wires were open to us to describe them, we duly reported them. In the outlying gardens and houses of Rasgrad, an important town in the centre of the Turkish line, lay fourteen victims of a barbarous deed : old

men, women, and children, Turkish natives of
Ablanova, a village not far away. Every one
of them was wounded with sabre, lance, or
bullet. A little girl of six had a sword-cut
on her head, a lance thrust in her side; her
mother, three cuts on the head and a bullet
in her thigh. The head of a middle-aged
woman was covered with wounds; on her
shoulder was a sabre - cut; in her side two
lance-thrusts; a boy of twelve had a gash in his
neck, and a ball through his body. There they
lay, the sole survivors, they said, of their village.
Questioned as to their assailants, it was the
Bulgars, they said, who fired their houses, but
the Moscov cavalry who wounded them; many
more women and children, they said, were killed
outright. That was all they could or would say,
and with that we had to be satisfied. No one
had seen the deed, but there, for all to see,
and puzzle over, was its result. The Political
Commission pointed triumphantly to these poor
maimed creatures and allowed fully detailed telegrams describing *this* " incident of war" to pass

L

the Censor. It was the only telegram which received such an honour. Whoever they were, Cossack, Russ, or Bulgar, the dastards who maimed these poor creatures, the fact of their maltreatment had to be chronicled. Of course the Sublime Porte made the most of it, and immediately invited diplomatic notice, so that the attention of Europe could be called to the horrors perpetrated by Christian assassins upon harmless Mussulman villagers. But the massacre of Ablanova was a *coup manqué*—nothing came of it; whereas the continuous record of Turkish atrocities, forwarded by the correspondents and military attachés who followed the Russian army, made Europe ring. In sight of the whole army Turkish cut-throats had come out of their forts and trenches and butchered the wounded on the glacis of Plevna, and " Pity ... striding the blast," had " blown the horrid deed in every eye "— without the assistance of Ambassadors.

Not long after the Ablanova affair there happened one of the frequent outpost skirmishes on the Lom, in which, according to the accounts

of the Turkish irregular cavalry (high-sounding
name for the Tcherkess and Bashi-Bazouk, scum
of the earth!) the Russians had been worsted.
I was in the neighbourhood when the victors
returned and interviewed one of the scoundrels.
"Yes," said the Bashi-Bazouk, with a grin, "the
Moscov ran, but we killed many.    They are too
heavy.   We can catch them.    Look! here is
their gun "—and he produced a Kranka rifle, a
breechloader with the Snider action ; heavy,
clumsy, ill-balanced ; a wretched weapon for a
mounted man, and as different as could be from
the handy little American-made Winchester
carbine which all the Turkish cavalry, regular
and irregular, carried.   Before the poor Russian
dragoon could get his unwieldly Kranka into play
his enemy could fire at least two rounds at him.
" Behold again, Effendi," said my Bashi-Bazouk,
" I will show you his horse."   A tall leggy steed
was trotted out for my inspection, differing from
the little Turkish Arab or Barb, much as the
rifles differed.   "And the rider," I asked, "What
of the rider ? "   " I killed the Moscov, Effendi,

and took his horse and gun; but that man over there has his breeches." I looked where he pointed, and there stood a Bashi-Bazouk, who was Bashi-Bazouk to his waist only; below that he was Russian dragoon, his legs having been forcibly thrust into tight cavalry breeches. One of the chiefest characteristics of the Bashi-Bazouk is that he is extremely baggy, and the aspect of this man was so comic that I laughed outright. All the bystanders joined in. No one had ever before seen a Bashi-Bazouk in tight breeches. I think the regiment with which these barbarians had been fighting was known as the Empress Catherine's Regiment of Dragoons. I bought the Russian horse and the Russian rifle. Had I wished to rescue the breeches I doubt whether their possessor could have got out of them.

# CHAPTER XII.

## War in the Happy Valley.

SOME day, perhaps, when free Bulgaria has done with political plots and the kidnapping of Princes, she will give to the world better proof that she has taken her place among civilized European nations by producing a Poet. A chapter upon Bulgarian literature just now would resemble a famous Chapter on Snakes. There is no literature in Bulgaria. But the material for it is there, hidden away in a mass of folk-lore from the days of Bulgarian Czars, who took no thought of Ottoman conquest, down through centuries of servitude, to the day when the Russian Czar struck the final blow—when Plevna fell, when Mehemet Ali struck *his* final blow (and broke his own neck) against the stone wall of the Czare-witch's army.

When the Bulgarian epic poet of the future shall have sung these things, and his country's deliverance, the pastoral poet, may be, shall arise and sing of his country's richness and beauty. He will issue, perhaps, from that delightful region, the Valley of the Lom, the little stream which, beginning in the Balkan, flows northward till it meets the Danube. It is small, and its course is short, but no rivulet in Europe flows through a lovelier valley. Girt round with high uplands and breezy downs, it has made itself a channel between little rocky cliffs, at the foot of which, through charming meadows, it rolls its tiny volume towards the great river, a humble tributary. It is the Slav Arcadia, this Valley of the Lom, and from it should come, some day, a man who will give Eastern Europe something better to think about than fat contracts for Berdan rifles, and the successful issue of national loans. Here, in this valley, with its little river, its fruit orchards, its timber-built, tile-roofed villages, a man might dream away his life in indolent peacefulness, "the world forgetting, by

the world forgot"; flowers all round his cottage,
a blue sky above, and a soil beneath so rich that,
with the slightest labour, it will yield bountiful
produce. Little lakes are formed here and there
by the running together of many springs, and, all
about, pastures for the cattle, rocks for the goats,
wide-stretching downs for horses.

Small wonder, then, that when the cavalry
outposts of the Czarewitch began to feel their
way towards the army of Mehemet Ali they
looked down with admiring wonder at the earthly
paradise beneath them. The Lom became the
debateable land of the two great hosts, between
which it flowed. On the eastern heights of the
valley lay the Turkish field army, concentrating
for its attempt to cut a way to Osman at Plevna;
on the western side the Russian army of the
Czarewitch, stretched out in a long line, faced
the Turks, determined to prevent any such
attempt. At any cost the attempt must be
defeated; Osman must be kept hemmed in without possibility of relief; the Russian covering
army must hold to the death the line of the Lom.

Alas for the inhabitants of the happy valley!
Time and again in those terrible days did the
fiery storm of war sweep up and down and across
it, leaving wrack and ruin behind. Those who
had seen it in the spring of 1877 scarce recognised it in the late summer, its gardens trampled,
its woods hewn, its houses shattered, its inhabitants
sadly thinned. The villagers who remained were
in constant terror lest the Russian should go and
the Turk should come; they gave up their houses
willingly enough when the Russian held the line;
they fled in panic when the Turk advanced.
Poor Bulgars of the Lom! It was a heavy price
that they paid for their liberty in that glorious
year of emancipation. Three full months had
passed since the declaration of war ere the storm-
cloud broke over their peaceful valley; the
Russians had been in undisturbed possession of
the line of the Lom for a month before sound
of rifle or cannon broke the stillness. When, at
last, the opposing hosts came to blows the fighting
was fast and fierce. It was not here, as at
Plevna, a matter of attacking a fixed position

week after week and month after month, but of
the manœuvring of armies in the field, of attack
and defence, advance and retreat, in the open
country ; and, although the Siege of Plevna over-
shadowed the Campaign of the Lom, the latter
was quite as interesting as a military operation.

It was towards the end of July that the first
round of the stand-up fight between the Czarewitch and Mehemet Ali was fought—the fierce
little battle of Esirdsché, remarkable for the fact
that the troops engaged on either side gave and
took volleys from breechloaders in the open at
a range of 150 yards ; hot work, which cost
the Turkish army its bravest soldier, Aziz
Pasha. The affair of Esirdsché was an accidental
encounter, in which, strange as it may seem, the
hostile forces stumbled upon one another ; it was
a surprise for both. Each side being, so to speak,
caught napping, fought with desperation to release
itself from unpleasant propinquity by dint of
sheer knocks. The whole Turkish army at that
time lay under the baneful spell of its late commander's indolence and incapacity ; the soldiers

were willing enough to fight, eager, indeed, to fight the accursed Giaour; but they had heard their officers openly express utter want of confidence in their chief. The army of 30,000 men lying on the heights about Rustchuk had been kept in a state of irritation. A few battalions would be told off for duty, and would march off in the direction of the Russian lines; they would encamp ten or fifteen miles from the fortress; then, without having struck a blow, march back again. The Marshal, Achmet Eyoub, was chiefly responsible for these singular operations.

Finally, when the Czarewitch had occupied without resistance the whole line of the Lom, and shut off the fortresses of Rustchuk and Shumla from the main line of invasion, the Marshal thought it was time to do something. So he detached a "force of observation" from the garrison of Rustchuk, large enough to observe, but too small to influence in the slightest degree the occupation by the Russians of the stragetic line so important to them. The "army of observation" did nothing; it did not even observe; and, after the usual camping out on the downs above the Lom Valley, it retired. The soldiers knew that across the river on the opposite heights lay the enemy, and they would have liked nothing better than to test the power of the Infidel to hold those heights. Listlessly they struck their tents, loaded up the baggage mules, and marched off back to their quarters under the guns of Rustchuk. The retreat was covered by three battalions, with two guns, under the command of Aziz. When this rear-guard was near the village of Esirdsché, the officer in charge of the flanking party came hurriedly in, and reported to Aziz that a large force of Russians was marching in a line parallel to his own, close by, just on the other side of a wood. "What nonsense," said Aziz, "there can be no Russians there;" and he began expostulating with the officer on his folly in imagining anything of the kind. Suddenly, from the edge of the wood, a rattling volley confirmed the officer's statement; a score of men, and Faizullah, the brigadier, went down before it. What did Aziz do? Concentrate the whole of his force and continue to retire, fighting, as a rear-guard should? Not a bit of it! One of his officers pointed to the overwhelming force of the enemy, and advised retreat. Aziz shot him dead with his revolver; then threw out half a battalion as skirmishers, and prepared to attack. Here, at last, was his opportunity to shake off the degrading yoke of craven indolence, and to show what an Ottoman commander could do. Amid a rifle fire, which swept through and through his little army, he brought his two guns into action, ordered the bugles to sound, placed himself at the head of the skirmish line, and advanced dauntlessly to the attack. Close behind their leader, the soldiers, fiercely shouting their war cry of "Allah! Allah!" dashed straight at the enemy. For a moment the Russian right wing shrank before the fury of the onslaught— but only for a moment. The gallant band, hopelessly overpowered, was lapped round with a circle of fire. Amid a hail of bullets, Aziz fell, shot through the head. His shattered force withdrew from the foolhardy enterprise, and the

Russians, who were quite as much astonished to find themselves fighting, made no further attempt to molest the rear-guard. Such was the combat of Esirdsché, one of the fiercest engagements of the war. It was said, afterwards, that Aziz deliberately courted his fate; he felt so keenly the disgraceful condition of the army that he had resolved to get himself killed on the battlefield at the first opportunity. Mehemet Ali arrived to take command during the same week in which Aziz was slain, and he felt keenly the loss of his gallant friend. The example of Aziz roused the whole army. No more indolent loafing behind fortresses now! Reorganisation, concentration, and a swift attack in force upon the Russian positions on the Lom—that was the order of the day.

Six weeks after the fight I passed over the battle ground. Once more I was in the Lom Valley, not now to linger and admire, but as a fugitive, weary, ill, starving, making the best of my way, in the rear of a beaten army, towards the shelter of the fortresses. The Russian

cavalry was pushing forward—I could see them
on the crest of the ridge behind—there was no
time to be lost, but I pulled up my horse for a
moment on the spot where the gallant Aziz fell.
Evidences of the fight were scattered thickly
around.  The shallow graves in which the dead
had been hastily buried had been scratched up
by the dogs and the vultures, and the corpses
devoured; bones and shreds of clothing lay all
about.  In the wood, and among the scrub oak,
were many terrible fragments of humanity which
had known no burial, and at which my horse
started and shied.  One of the skulls had a little
round hole, with sharp clean edges, in the centre
of the forehead.  The sickening smell of a battle
field poisoned the air.  A hideous spot, a
Golgotha, the once charming neighbourhood of
Esirdsché—a place to hurry past and to forget.
Vast fields of wheat and barley were still uncut,
the grain dropping from the ear.  Here and
there a few skulking peasants were attempting
to save a portion of their harvest; in a few hours
the pursuing cavalry would occupy the village

and would certainly requisition their scanty sheaves.

As I turned to look once more from the top of the next ridge, the reapers had vanished; there was no sign of life anywhere in the plain. Beyond, against the skyline, were the advancing spears of the Cossacks. Alas for the happy valley !

# CHAPTER XIII.

## At Close Quarters with the Czarewitch.

IT took Mehemet Ali, with all his European energy, a full month to prepare his army for the great event—the attempt to break through the covering force of the Czarewitch's army. A month lost in war time, as in time of peace, was a small matter to that stupid old Oriental, Abdul Kerim, who now lay in durance vile in Constantinople awaiting his trial, but it needed no stimulus from the Sublime Porte to keep the new commander up to the mark. He carried out his instructions to force the fighting. The death of Aziz, in the rear-guard engagement at Esirdsché did more to stir up the Turkish field army than Iradés or special missions of secret councillors. The rank and file of the forty thousand men with whom Mehemet Ali was about to strike his blow were ready for action, and when, finally, the concentration was complete, it became evident that the plan was to strike at the Russian right wing from the town of Eski Djuma, and then at the centre from Rasgrad.

Towards the end of August the commander arrived at Eski Djuma, and with him came a full staff of officers and aides-de-camps, among them Valentine Baker, our own gallant ex-colonel of hussars, who for one moment of madness was paying the bitter penalty of perpetual exile. Here he was, now, a Pasha, with the Ottoman fez on his head, once better graced with the English busby, but still the same quiet-mannered keen-eyed soldier. Baker was heartily welcomed by Mehemet Ali, who had asked him to come to the front, but he brought along with him the whole of the English staff of the " gendarmerie," among them Colonel Briscoe, formerly of the 15th Hussars, and Major Allix, formerly of the Grenadiers. Besides these came Sartorius, Swire, Drummond, Prime, and Annesley, and the military attachés, Colonel Lenox, V.C.,

M

Captain Chermside, and Captain de Torcy, of
the French Army.    The headquarters of the
Turkish army thus suddenly became more
English than Turkish, and the Bulgarian spies
who crossed into the Russian lines must have
considerably astonished their friends with
accounts of the "English invasion."    What the
effect of the news was on the Russian commanders we had no means of knowing, but the
effect upon the Turkish commander was evident.
He regarded the deluge of English with something like consternation.    What was he, the
Commander of the army of the Faithful, to do
with all these infidels?    They wore the same
uniform as he did, and he could not offer them
any slight; but what would his rivals, Suleïman
at Shipka and Osman at Plevna, say to it?    The
presence of the English contingent was the
means of revealing to us the real secret of the
inherent rottenness of the Turkish Empire.

These three men who had in their hands its
destinies, Mehemet Ali, Suleiman, and Osman,
were, one and all, animated by the same senti-

ments ; each one of them hated the Russians and desired to beat them, each one of them hated the other two and hoped most fervently that they would fail. Suleiman, it was notorious, fought for his own hand in the Shipka Pass ; he did his best to win his own battles and to prevent Mehemet Ali from deriving any benefit from them. He would not come through the Balkans (as he might have done with the greatest ease at any time) and join his chief in striking at the Czarewitch's line ; his "interests" lay in uselessly hammering away at the pass which the Russians held ; Mehemet's plans were Mehemet's business, not his. The Sublime Porte, in its suicidal sublimity, turned a deaf ear to Mehemet's entreaties, and did not order Suleiman to obey his superior officer, but patted him on the back for his "glorious defence of the Shipka Pass," and told Mehemet Ali to carry out his own combinations. With whom he was to combine was a question which the Sublime Porte did not trouble itself.

Thus ambition at the front and intrigue in the

Palace destroyed the finest opportunity a commander ever had to crush his country's enemies.
That with Suleiman's army added to his own
Mehemet Ali could have raised the siege of
Plevna, is as certain as anything can be. Upon
Suleiman and his powerful friends at Court rests
the responsibility for the failure of a campaign
that began brilliantly and fizzled out igno-
miniously. Within a month from the time that
poor Mehemet undertook his enterprise alone the
last hope of holding the Russians in Northern
Bulgaria was gone. The attack on the Czarewitch
having died away, Osman was squeezed in a
tighter grip ; when Plevna fell the Shipka Pass
was turned and the road to Constantinople was
open.

Mehemet Ali set to work, with his mixed
headquarters staff, to carry out the plan of
attack, and Eski Djuma was the centre of
activity such as it has never known before or
since. The iron hand of war lay heavy on the
little town. One of the most famous fairs in the
East of Europe is held there annually. Immense

quantities of merchandise are landed at Rustchuk and sent on by rail and waggon, and in the great square might be seen merchants from Constantinople, Asia Minor, and even Persia. You could buy Yankee petroleum, Marseilles sugar, Viennese glass, German clocks, and Rodgers's cutlery, in the booths of this remote little Balkan town. There was no fair now; the great square was choked with ammunition waggons and the baggage train of a large army; no buyers and sellers thronged the streets; the houses were shut; it was almost impossible to get a lodging in the town. The Turk's house is, of course, always closed to a Christian stranger, and the Bulgarian was almost as shy; but for a different reason. The Turk objected to strangers at his gate on religious grounds; the Bulgar did not wish anyone to see how comfortable he was amid all the surrounding misery. For no less than 60,000 semi-starved Turkish families, fugitives from the Danube bank, from Sistova, Tirnova, and the Jantra valley, were camped in the fields about the town. How these poor creatures kept

alive while the army, in addition to the usual
population, was eating up the country, was a
mystery to us.   Many hundreds, probably, died
in their quiet resigned Turkish way, yielding to
destiny and making no fuss about it.   But the
Bulgar of Eski Djuma had evidently taken
thought for the morrow, and could quietly bide
his time until the war was over, without any
danger of starvation.   Those who were fortunate
enough to obtain an entrance into the houses
of the wealthier Bulgarian inhabitants were
astonished to find charming rooms, lined with
beautiful woodwork, out of which they could
step into delightful little gardens perfumed with
flowers and tinkling with tiny fountains.

By the end of August the Turkish field army
was concentrated in two masses, at Rasgrad and
at Eski Djuma, and their outposts on the line
between these two towns faced the army of the
Czarewitch holding the line of the Lom.   The
Russians had remained in undisturbed possession
of their positions ever since the passage of the
Danube, and had masked the fortresses of the

Quadrilateral, shutting them off from the main
line of invasion through Bulgaria from the
Danube to the Balkan, and covering the rear
of the great army which was besieging Plevna.
The Czarewitch's army was thus a defensive
screen, behind which lay the broad belt of country
already conquered by the invaders. Osman at
Plevna was a thorn in the other side, but he was
ringed round with fire and steel in his impregnable position, and could not move. Mehemet
Ali determined to break through the Czarewitch's
army, strike at the Russian line of communications, and relieve Osman. Had Suleiman
joined him, the Turkish army would have out-
numbered the Russians, and the bold plan would
almost certainly have succeeded; but Suleiman
would not help his rival to the seals of the Grand
Vizierate, for which these two patriotic commanders were struggling, and Mehemet had to
make the attempt alone. He and the Czarewitch
were evenly matched; they could each bring
about forty thousand men into the field; but the
advantage lay with the Turk, for he had collected

his fighting army into two compact masses, and
could hurl them—as he did—against the thin
line of the enemy, which was stretched over
nearly fifty miles of country.

The 12th and 13th Russian Corps formed this
line, the 35th division being that which directly
faced the Turkish army at Eski Djuma. The
Russian positions along this line were everywhere
close to the River Lom, whose well-defined
valley was the boundary between the armies;
but towards the south, opposite Eski Djuma,
where Mehemet Ali now was, the valley is
dominated by a high plateau, the possession of
which was absolutely necessary to the Turks.
But the Russians were there, and had been there
for weeks. With the struggle for this commanding position the offensive movement for the relief
of Plevna began.

Valentine Baker was the leading spirit in the
three days' fighting for the possession of the
plateau. It was mere outpost fighting, in which
the numbers were few and the losses slight, but
the style in which the operation was conducted

was masterly, and the Russians, who had remained so long in indolent possession of the
position, must have been extremely surprised at
the manner in which they were hustled into the

VALENTINE BAKER.

valley on the third day. Three times did they
attempt to regain their hold; once they actually
did regain it; but Baker was not to be denied,
and the Turkish infantry, fully realising that they
were being led by a soldier, showed themselves

immensely superior in fighting power to the Russians. I can see Valentine Baker now, as he sat outside his tent in the camp of Sarnasuflar on the heights of the Lom ; unwilling ever to talk much about his success, but, when he did talk, so quiet, so self-possessed, so unconscious of his own skill and his own valour. Every inch a soldier and a gentleman was Valentine Baker. The recollection of that strange and terrible moment of his past, which terminated his career as an English officer, never impaired the esteem of those who knew him in his exile. When the remembrance of it arose, there arose with it a feeling of incredulity that *this* man, so courteous, so kindly, so brave, could be *that* man so——— what the British jurymen said he was. Anyhow, I, who knew him well, am content to remember him only as an officer and a gentleman.

The three days' battle for the plateau was over, and two remarkable incidents of it remain fixed in my memory : the fate of the " Polish Legion," and the fact that the Turkish army could actually point to three Russian prisoners of war. Three wretched-looking beings they were, ragged, thin, despondent, but (and this was the most surprising fact to us and to them) alive! For in this fighting for the Lom, as in the fighting at Plevna, and everywhere else where Turk met Russian, it was "no quarter." Murder stalked behind Victory. The path of a conquering Turkish army was strewn with dismembered corpses, whose heads, often their hands and feet, were hacked off. Sometimes indignities still more shocking had been inflicted on the bodies, and, where time did not permit of these barbarities, the throats of the helpless wretches who lay in the line of advance were cut from ear to ear. Standing, once, close behind the fighting line in one of the desperate combats of those three days, during which the Russians were gradually pushed off the plateau, I saw three wounded Russians crawl beneath a tree for shelter from the burning sun. Presently the Turkish line advanced, and I saw a man stop at the tree, and deliberately cut the throats, one after another, of every mother's son. It was done in a twinkling. Next moment the assassin had rejoined his comrades and went on with them as they raged through the crackling rifle-fire which burst from the bush in their front, careless of the hissing shells which tore their ranks. The fierce war shout of "Allah" was on their lips, and murder, for their God's sake, was in their hearts. A terrible picture, never to be effaced from my mind!

Thus it was that the living presence of those three poor fellows in the Turkish camp was a source of astonishment to us. They were sitting there on a rude bench outside one of the huts, on the evening of their capture, the centre of a group of Turkish soldiers. As I went up to see what was going on, I saw that their lives hung by a thread, and that the fate which had over-taken their wounded comrades in the field was imminent over them here. For some of the Turks were jeering at them, and laughing at their plight; others regarded them with a steady stare of intense hate. It was clear that the passion of the crowd was rising; the sight of these accursed Giaours was goading them to madness. Some of the fierce eyes were turned on me. I unbuttoned the flap of my revolver. Presently a man stepped up to one of the prisoners, seized him by the chin, and, with a grin of scorn, spat in his face. In another moment knives would be out, and it would be too late.

I ran into the hut of one of the English surgeons and called him. The sight of his uniform checked the excitement at once. In another moment a Turkish officer arrived, and when we had explained the matter to him he fell to cuffing the men as if they were a parcel of schoolboys bullying some weak lad, and accompanied each blow with a volley of Turkish curses which sounded terrific. The men scattered and fled, laughing and chattering, and thus what bid fair to be a hideous tragedy ended in merriment. The three poor prisoners were at once carted off to Rasgrad. In course of time, maybe, they got back to Russia, and I daresay they have thought, now and again, of the Englishmen who saved their lives.

In that same battle the Polish Legion received
its baptism of fire, expiring immediately there-
after.    Unfortunate Polish Legion!    At the
beginning of the war the Porte had issued a
proclamation announcing it was prepared to enrol
Poles for service against their ancient enemy,
and would place 100 guns and forty thousand
stand of arms at their disposal.    The result of
the proclamation was that there stood in battle
array with the army of Mehemet Ali exactly
*forty-six* Poles!    They were up at the front in
the fight for the Lom position, and, strangely
enough, one of the very first Russian shells that
were fired on the first day, burst right in front
of them, killing and wounding fifteen men.    Four
days after, when the wounded were brought
into Eski Djuma, I was passing between the
rows of poor fellows who lay on the heaps of
straw in the Bulgarian school-house.    One of
them beckoned to me, and, when he found I
understood French, made a motion with his hand
towards the blanket which covered his legs,
and said, "Regardez, Monsieur."    I raised the

blanket.  One of his feet had just been amputated; the other was shattered, and mortification
had already extended up above the knee.   He
was an intelligent, well-educated young fellow,
and told me that he was a Pole, and had once
been connected with a Polish newspaper in
London.

"Now I am dying here," he went on;
"and the man who cut off my foot was an
apothecary; not one of your English surgeons—
ah no!—the man *hacked* it off, and would not
touch the other; and you see it is now too
late."

I fetched one of the English doctors to see
him, and the poor fellow's own diagnosis of his
case was confirmed; it *was* too late.   We could
do nothing for him.

Later, I prepared and took him a bottle of
Liebig's extract.   After talking a while, he said,
" Raise me a little, Monsieur."

I passed my arm round his back and raised
him.

"You are kind to me, Monsieur," he said,

with a smile; and then with a shuddering
sigh he dropped his head on my shoulder
and died.

Some of his colleagues and a few of us English
followed him to his grave. A Winchester carbine
box, with one end knocked out to make room
for his poor maimed legs, did duty as his coffin.

# CHAPTER XIV.

## 𝔄 𝔏ittle 𝔏ull.

THE arm-chair war correspondents who sat at home at ease, and, by collating official despatches from the front, evolved articles upon the " Progress of the War," had plenty to say about the new phase of the campaign which was opened by Mehemet Ali on the Lom. Unfortunately for the public, what they said was mainly rubbish.

" If," remarked one of these gentlemen, who had no doubt closely followed the news from the front with the aid of a large map, conveniently suspended on the wall, so that he could contemplate it without moving from the fire or taking his hands from under his coat-tails—"if Mehemet Ali has 100,000 men, he ought to be cashiered for not using them ; if he has fewer than that number he ought to be cashiered for doing what he seems to be doing." This and much more to the same effect emanated from the newspaper Von Moltkes, who guided the British public amid the maze of the Bulgarian battlefields, or described the moves on the vast chess-board of the war. Probably each of these strategists thought that he, and he only, had the whole thing at his fingers' ends, and that could he, by touching a bell, set armies in motion—as was the proud boast of the American war-secretary at the beginning of the great Civil War—the campaign would be speedily ended. Thus the Tory arm-chair strategist saw plainly how by *his* combinations the Russians could be hurled back into the Danube and drowned; while the Radical, leaning back, complacent, in cushioned seat, settled the fate of the Turkish Empire entirely to *his* satisfaction. Not one of these gentlemen, Turco-phil or Turko-phobe, realised that the *basis* of his calculations was, chiefly, lies, and that his conclusions were therefore false. A single hour in Valentine Baker's tent at headquarters would have destroyed the arguments by which the writers of the war-summaries in the London daily papers elaborately proved, in several columns of print, that $2 - 1 = 2$.

We, at the front, when the postal authorities delivered our journals to us (as they did, once in awhile), laughed heartily over these lucubrations. Our views of the campaign were not quite so comprehensive, to be sure; we could get no bird's-eye view (from a convenient distance); our despatches were written in tents, in the saddle, in the interior of field-works while the guns were in action and the enemy's shells bursting just on the other side of a few feet of earth. We could describe only what we saw. And we were always quite certain that $2 + 2 = 4$. Thus we knew quite well, at the very beginning of the Turkish attempt to break the line of the Czarewitch, that Mehemet Ali had *not* 100,000 men; and we knew also why, with less than half that number, he was doing what he was.

Well, then, if we knew it, why did we not say it? There are several answers to the question,

but the most conclusive of them will suffice:
It is not a desirable termination to the career of
a war-correspondent to be led out, with bandaged
eyes, to be stood with his back to a rock, and
there to be shot as a spy. We knew that
Suleiman, who kept his army on the other side
of the Balkans, and banged his head against
the Schipka Pass to no purpose, was doing it
for his own glory; we knew that he would not
march through the easy passes on the east and
join us, because he would have no hand in
making his colleague famous; we knew that the
*combined* army could have cut right through
the weak Russian brigades echelonned between
Rasgrad and Tirnova, and compelled the raising
of the siege of Plevna; but the single sentence
which would have conveyed all this, namely,
"*Suleiman Pasha is a traitor to his country,*"
could not be said or written. And so the
cushioned Von Moltkes were at sea, and their
editorial summaries were so much waste paper.

The journalistic moral of all this is: first, not
to write "war summaries" in the office chair;

second, to take "official despatches" with a grain
of salt; and, last, to be content with the best
that the accredited man at the front can do;
remembering always that, being kicked and
cuffed and bullied by the army with which he
serves (besides being shot at by the enemy), he
*cannot* say very much that is of strategical
importance to his paper; and that what is
of strategical importance to himself—namely,
running away—he *must not* do. Such are my
sentiments,—the result of practical experience,
as to war correspondence and the editing of a
daily paper during a great war.

It was not until the three days' fight for the
high plateau on the right bank of the Upper
Lom had resulted in the dislodging of the
Russian outposts, that we, who were there, got
a clear idea of the intentions of Mehemet Ali
and Valentine Baker. The brilliant manner in
which our English ex-colonel of Hussars had
handled his men, and the evident share which
he had in the Turkish councils of war, became
speedily known throughout the Turkish field

army. The war correspondents came flocking into Eski Djuma—English, French, German, Austrian.

Poor Mehemet Ali, who had been frightened by the deluge of English officers, was now appalled by the avalanche of pressmen, but he made the best of it, and, instead of bullying and insulting us as his predecessor had done, he assumed an attitude of friendly reserve. "Wait, messieurs, till I am ready, and then you shall see"—that was his stock phrase for his interviewers. Valentine Baker's tent was, of course, the point of attraction for the English portion of the Press-brigade, and most of them got very much the same advice from him—"Wait and you will see."

To me, whom he knew, and whose brother had been aide-de-camp to him in many a field day at Aldershot, Baker was a little less non-committal, perhaps; but the natural and proper caution of a soldier in the field was relaxed, even in my case, only so far as to say, at the time when the words had a meaning in them, "I should think that you had better be as near headquarters as you conveniently can, to-morrow."

The morrow's rising sun would find me and my faithful Uhlan mounted and ready in the closest possible proximity to headquarters, with a certainty of seeing battalions under arms marching off in the direction of the enemy, and of hearing, not long after, the spatter of rifle fire and the ringing crack of the Krupps. Thus it was that I witnessed the desperate series of skirmishes in those wooded heights—the key to the whole position on the Upper Lom—the seizure of which was the first evidence that Mehemet Ali meant business, and that the Czarewitch's army would have to stand up and fight him. How the Turkish general fared in his attempt; how, with only half the force he had calculated upon having at his disposal, he not only made the Czarewitch fight hard, but even caused the Czar himself to think of packing up and moving his headquarters a little further back, I shall attempt to tell.

But, meanwhile, after the capture of the

heights, there was a lull of a few days, during which the final preparations were completed. The next advance would be across the river, and the whole army would be sent straight at the Czarewitch's right and centre. There was some good reason for the delay beside the usual Oriental habit of procrastination, but it was difficult to ascertain it precisely; it lay somewhat in the commissariat. The Turkish soldier does not want much. He will march and fight all day on a handful of corn or rice and a cup of water; tinned provisions are unknown to him, and his camp kettle rarely contains anything but a mess of vegetables at which Tommy Atkins would sniff with the utmost disdain. For months the army had been lying in the district, with nothing to do but to parade and sleep and eat, and the country was almost exhausted. It happened more than once that the Commander-in-Chief received a telegram from his depôt at Rasgrad stating that only one day's fodder remained for the horses of the cavalry and artillery. The hitch in the offensive operations was not taken advantage of by the Russians, who, indeed, seemed to be quite as familiar as the Turks with the noble Oriental proverb, " Never do to-day what you can put off till to-morrow." The Czarewitch did not strengthen his right wing after losing the heights of the Upper Lom, and when the Turkish commander, having got his provisions together, advanced in force the Russian right wing was instantly smashed.

Meanwhile, strange sights and scenes met us in and about Eski Djuma, and strangest of all was the attitude of Bulgarian to Turk and Turk to Bulgarian. For news had filtered to us through the Balkan passes that in Adrianople they were hanging and shooting the Bulgars by thousands. It was an exaggeration, of course. Seven Bulgars who had tried to blow up the railway with dynamite had been caught and strung up to a tree; thirty more had been executed for rape and pillage; and, here and there, when they were caught carrying informa- tion to the enemy—a thing they all did if they got a chance—they were shot or hanged by twos and threes. The thrifty inhabitants of Eski Djuma pondered well these things and "lay low." Wise Bulgars! for they were in parlous state. A great army, every man of which loathed and despised them, lay camped in and around their town, and three events had recently roused the Turks to such a pitch that, at the slightest word, streets would have run blood, and houses would have been swept away like chaff. The death of the gallant Aziz, the declaration of war by Roumania, and the Sultan's general call to arms—these were as so many red rags to a bull. The Bulgar kept out of sight, and awaited behind his door or in his cellar the hour of deliverance, when the Czar-matador should give the mortal thrust.

I had something to say about Turkish surgery in the case of the young Pole who died so sadly. We saw in those few days in the Turkish hospitals deeds so barbarous, so brutal, that the most obtuse of Tories would have found some reason to reconsider his favourite phrase, " The Turk is such a gentleman, you know." See this hospital in the Bulgarian school-house, in which lie the wounded; long rows of patient creatures in dire need of skilled surgery, and not a surgeon there save one or two Englishmen who were hampered in every attempt to relieve suffering. The wounded, on arrival, after hours spent in the hot sun, jolting in the rough country carts, were shot out into the courtyard. There was no one to receive them. But for the two English doctors and two of us pressmen who went out to buy them food, many of them would have died then and there. They were grateful, these poor maimed creatures, to the infidels who brought them bread and water-melons and cigarettes. But many of them were beyond all help of surgery, and past caring for the things of earth. There were men who had lain where they fell, in the burning sun of day, in the chill dews of night, for thirty-six mortal hours. Then, when at last they were picked up, they were brought to the town in springless country carts, shaken and jolted over twelve long miles of rough country. And their wounds! With a shudder

I recall the aspect of the ghastly hurts that were revealed when we set to work with lint and bandage; rended flesh, shattered bone, and—horror of horrors!—maggots. Even the doctors turned sick and faint. Burning with indignation we carried the suffering wretches into the school-house, laid them on heaps of straw, and then set off to report to the authorities that they were there. Presently some of the officials, whatever they were, apothecaries or horse-doctors, came and—thanked us for what we had done? Not at all; they abused us for having interfered.

"Look here," said one of the English doctors, "some of these cases require immediate attention; this man, here, you see his arm—it should be amputated at once."

"It cannot be," said the Turkish medicine-man; "no amputation can be permitted without a special order from headquarters."

"But headquarters are fifteen miles away, and you see that the wound has been neglected; the man will die to-night if his arm is not taken off now."

"It cannot be ; our religion forbids dismemberment."

" Then you will let the man die ? "

" If God wills it, he will die." Die he did,
and many a brave fellow with him, that same
night—murdered by the Koran. It was as well,
perhaps, since they would not allow our surgeons
to operate, that they did not operate themselves ;
the patients' fate would then have been the same,
for the Turkish medicine-man was incompetent
to perform the most trivial operation ; he was
a mere dresser of wounds, an apothecary, with
much the same knowledge of medicine that his
ancestors had centuries ago, and barred by the
religion of his ancestors from all knowledge of
surgery. How many hundreds or thousands of
men were thus done to death, and with what
tortures, none can tell ; but everywhere, on every
battle-field, in every hospital, torture and death
were endured and faced by the wounded Turks
with the most heroic fortitude, and by the aid
of that self-same religion which decreed both.
Remarkable religion ! remarkable race !

Other things happened during the lull in the campaign, things comic as well as things tragic, for the drama of war is a drama of tears and laughter.    Take this little nocturnal scene for instance.    Eski Djuma is quiet; the streets are, as usual, silent and empty; the last bugle sounded long ago from the camp of the reserves outside; even the correspondents—restless beings—are abed.    Suddenly a distant rifle shot breaks the stillness; then another; then a perfect splutter of musketry.    Presently a war correspondent comes running down the street to the house where several more of us lodged.

"I say, you fellows, get up, there's something wrong!"

Up we jump and open shutters.

"What is it?"

"Listen!"    A roar of musketry, now, in the town and out of it.

"A night attack by the Russians!"

"A massacre of the Bulgarians!"    Some shouted one thing, some another; all began dressing, pulling on boots, strapping on revolvers.

Then we hurried into the street. At the door stood our Bulgar host, calm and collected.

" Do not disturb yourselves, gentlemen," said he, "it is nothing."

" Nothing! Why, don't you hear the firing ?"

" I hear it ; but look at the moon, gentlemen, look at the moon."

We looked, and behold the moon was eclipsed.

The Turkish army was firing at the Monster that was eating the Moon.

## CHAPTER XV.

## Before the Attack.

"YES," said Valentine Baker, with his quiet smile, in answer to my anxious questioning, " I think you will have time to ride in to Shumla and post your letters; but I should be back here on or about the 30th, if I were you." It was then the evening of the 27th August, and all had been quiet at the front since the capture of the heights of Kiritchen above the Lom. But the Turkish headquarters' staff was very busy, night and day, preparing for the next move. That evening a Krupp gun had been hauled up to the very summit of the highest hill of the ridge, the Sakar Tepé, and the artillerymen had tested its power upon a battalion of Russian infantry in the plain below. The shell dropped into the middle of them, and evidently caused

considerable surprise. They did not know that
a gun was there, high above them, and the fact
must have brought perturbation to the mind of
the Russian general, as he looked up at the lost
ridge, impregnable now though he had twenty
times his force. "We shall have a whole battery
up there before you come back," said Baker to
me as I bid him *au revoir* and set off, my own
postman, to Shumla, where the postal " bureau "
was established. "Every man his own postman"
was the rule for us, and many a hard ride, many
a sleepless night, did it involve. Unless we
handed in our letters ourselves there was no
certainty that they would ever reach their destina-
tion, and as the telegraph was practically closed
to us except for "inspired" messages, there was
nothing for it but to ride the thirty miles, up hill
and down dale, from the front to Eski Djuma
and thence to Shumla.

A charming country it is to ride through, and
my colleague and I lingered on the road to enjoy
the lovely prospects of mountain and valley
which met us at every turn. Our little cavalcade

O

was imposing—masters in front, servants behind,
all armed to the teeth, and for rear-guard an
araba or country cart laden with provisions and
baggage, and driven by a Turkish arabajee. It
is necessary to be imposing and to swagger a bit
in a country where a threat must be backed by
visible means of carrying it out, and the hand
never raised without giving the blow. The
whole district was infested with prowling Circassians and Bashi-Bazouks, who were not at all
particular as to the throats they cut, provided
they were the throats of Giaours. A cheerful
readiness to use, at a moment's notice, the newest
pattern of revolver, is the best possible frame of
mind to be in on meeting these gentry. It saves
misunderstanding.

Thus we went our way unmolested, and, after
our sixty-mile ride was over, found ourselves
safe in our skins (albeit with less skin than when
we started) with little to chronicle save our
impressions of the delightful scenery. We
feasted our eyes, tired with long vistas of tents
and the squalid sights of camp life, upon the

enchanting landscape; we watched, as we rode, the changing shadows rush over hill and valley, as welcome clouds floated now and again across the burning sun. For miles we would pass over undulating hills, and then come to little ravines, whose steep sides were clothed with thick woods already beginning to show the changing hues of late summer; or the road would be overhung by bold masses of grey rock, amid which, at one place, we noticed a cave, high overhead, with strange window-like slits on either side of the entrance—some Byzantine hermit's cell, maybe; a little beyond, the sides of the valley were clothed with grape-laden wild vines, whose thick clusters would be ready in another fortnight for the thirsty throat of the wayfarer; intermingled with the vines the wild passion flower grew, and groves of hazel-nut trees flourished here and there. A charming country! free from all sight and sound of strife, but reminding us, by its very loneliness, that grim-visaged war was scowling upon it and frightening away the simple folk whose dwelling-place it was. A single

Bashi-Bazouk who had picketed his horse and was busy among the bushes making a raid upon the nuts, was the only human being we came upon until we got to the Shumla Pass. Here we met a vehicle full of Turkish women, all, of course, huddled up in shapeless draperies and closely yashmakked. With them was their lord and master. He gave us no friendly looks as we passed. The meeting was evidently a source of amusement to our servants. My companion's Albanian made remarks of an ambiguous nature to our Turkish driver; there were mysterious headshakings and incomprehensible bursts of laughter. Not long after we heard a loud yell from the top of the pass behind us, and on galloping back to our caravan a woful sight broke upon us. There lay our cart, wheels up, the horses standing fifty yards away, and all our belongings scattered about among the bushes overhanging the precipice. A red stream issuing from beneath the cart told a tale, not of a slain driver (for there he sat on the ground, contemplating the wreck) but of broken bottles. All our

precious "Carlowitz" was running away! To pitch
man and cart over, and complete the annihilation
of our baggage train, was our first furious
thought, but the arabajee disarmed our resent-
ment. Picking himself up he began to talk to
himself and at himself in an astonishing manner.
" I knew it," he said, "Ah, I knew it. I expected
it from the very moment. I was sure it would
happen the very instant we saw that araba full
of——(then came some highly uncomplimentary
allusions to the ladies we had met), and I knew
we should not finish our journey in peace. The
women did it." " Why the devil didn't you keep
awake and drive straight?" said we. But he only
went on feebly diving about among the litter,
and repeating " The women did it." We left him
there with the assurance that if he did not get
into the town by sundown we should hand him
over to the Pasha to be whipped.

Our letters posted, we hurried back to headquarters, not lingering on the return journey, but
thinking only of those Krupps which ought now
to be on the mountain, ready at the signal to

hurl destruction on the plain. We rode our back
track of thirty miles with only one adventure. A
mile beyond the fortress, my comrade, riding
ahead, was suddenly challenged by a picket of
Turkish infantry. He had no pass. The soldiers
drew up across the road; one of them seized his
bridle. I gallop up. "What is this?" I ask.
"You go no further; you have no pass." I im-
pressively draw from my pocket the document
mentioned in the first article of this series. It is
the size of a piece of note paper. I slowly unfold
it till it is as big as a napkin—the soldiers let go
of our bridles. The document increases to the
size of a hearthrug—the picket falls back. With
a final shake it becomes a table-cloth, and in the
corner glitters the golden seal as big as a plate.
"Pass, Effendi, pass!" says the frightened ser-
geant, and the whole guard present arms to the
"Friends of the Sultan," as we sweep by in
stately procession.

Without further adventure we arrived at the
front at sundown on the 29th—the eve of the
eventful day. Tired as we were, we were roused

by the stirring sights and scenes in the camp;
trumpets were sounding, thousands of men were
falling in by companies and by battalions; in front
of the tent of the Commander-in-Chief a band
was playing (in various dispersed keys) a selec-
tion from "La Belle Hélène" (Offenbach here
in the Bulgarian mountains!), to which Mehemet
proudly invited us to listen. In front of the
tents the headquarters' staff was chatting—Prince
Hassan, of the Egyptian Contingent, gorgeous
in long yellow boots, Valentine Baker, Colonel
Lenox, V. C., Captain de Torcy, and, a new
arrival, Mr. Ashbury, M.P. To-morrow's battle
was the theme. Everything was ready; the
battery was planted on the height of the Sakar
Tepé; the troops were taking up their positions;
Nedjib Pasha and his 20,000 men at Rasgrad
had their orders.

And the Russians? Well, they quite understood
the importance of our position on these heights,
and must have known that the portion of the
ridge, and the village of Karahassan, to which
they clung, were untenable. Several weeks

before the advance movement of Mehemet Ali the Czarewitch had ordered their occupation, and, as the Turkish field army was then peacefully sleeping and eating under the *régime* of old Abdul Kerim, the operation was not a difficult one—a skirmish or two, some outpost scrimmages, and then a few battalions of the 35th Division of the Russian army settled themselves comfortably on these commanding positions of the Upper Lom, which, had they been so minded, would have secured a line for offensive operations against Shumla and the other fortresses of the quadrilateral. Osman at Plevna paralyzed any such intention ; every available man was wanted there.

The warning voice of the Krupp field-piece from the mountain top had no effect, and the Czarewitch's advanced posts contented themselves with watching the Turkish pickets—tedious enough business, if we may judge from the accounts which the correspondents who were with the Russians gave of their visits to the Russian front on the Lom.

My friend, Frank Millet, well known as a painter now, was, in those days, one of the war correspondents in Bulgaria, with the Russians; and when we came to compare notes in England, after the war, we found that he and I were many a time in close proximity to each other, staring through our field-glasses from the hostile camps, wondering whether there were any colleagues behind the outposts, whose camp fires fringed the woods by night, and whose cavalry vedettes we could see dodging about by day. Pleasant would it have been to have popped across and had a chat; but we might as well have been on opposite sides of the wide world as on opposite banks of that Bulgarian rivulet.

Millet was busy with his pen over there, among the thatched houses of Karahassan, describing the *dolce far niente* of life with the Russian outposts; and I, within cannon-shot, was equally busy telling how very shortly we proposed to advance in force and sweep the Russians, bag and baggage, off the heights and out of the village. Not long after, we were

within rifle shot of each other, I with the triumphant Turk raging amid the carnage of the
assault, he flying for his life amid the shattered
remnants of Leonoff's brigade.

But as yet all was quiet, and amid Millet's
writings there was no hint that he or anyone
else in the Russian camp realized the importance of strengthening their hold upon the
heights.

" Leonoff conducted me," says Millet, " to his
quarters among the straw stacks around the
village, and we made ourselves comfortable under
the great walnut trees. The hussars built me
a charming little hut of sticks and straw, the
General lived in a shelter tent hard by. We ate
beneath the trees, and if the nuts did not drop
fairly into our hands we had only to throw up a
stick to knock them off. For days we watched
the white ponies of the Circassian outposts of the
Turkish army, whisking about the edge of the
wood; we planned reconnaissances up to the
railway; we examined the fortifications on the
heights above Rasgrad. General Vannoffsky,

the Chief of the Czarewitch's staff, came himself and inspected our position. Yonder in the maize fields twenty or thirty dead Turks, killed in a recent skirmish, still lay, and we sent out a burying party to cover them with earth. We could see the enemy's outposts by day, and their camp fires by night, but they seemed to have no intention of attacking, and we began to find life at the outposts not so full of incident after all. We had in the village of Karahassan only one regiment, the Zaraiskie, No. 140, counting not more than 2,500 men, one battery of artillery, two big guns, and 500 cavalry. With this force it was out of the question to attempt to get possession of the whole of the ridge, and so we were obliged to content ourselves with watching the movements of the Turks. But last Thursday morning the eagles which had been circling over the corpses in the maize fields were seen high in the air above the Valley of the Lom, and General Leonoff said this was an infallible sign of an imminent action."

Right, Augur Leonoff! You rightly read the flight of the royal birds; for even now, behind those whisking outposts, behind those camp fires, an army is gathered for your destruction. Before the eagles have left the sky the dogs of war, straining in the leash, will be let slip upon you!

# CHAPTER XVI.

## The Fight for the Lom.

"WE shall attack in force to-morrow." That
was the final decision at the council of
war on the Kiritchen heights, as the sun sank
below the wide, undulating plain, over which we
had looked so often and so eagerly in those last
days of August. It was the evening of the 29th,
and, as the welcome twilight descended, the
members of Mehemet Ali's headquarters' staff
strolled off to their tents to get as long a night as
possible before the morrow's business. "We
shall attack in force" meant business. For six
weeks the Turkish commander had been preparing himself for this *mot d'ordre*, and now, at
last, we were on the eve of the eventful day.
From morning till night of this day before the
battle the woods had been alive with troops

marching to take up their positions ; the artillery
had been pulled, and pushed, and hoisted through
the brushwood, over the rocks, and up to the
very top of the Sakar mountain.   Three Krupps
were planted there ; below them, on the edge of
a plateau, stood a full battery, and on the slope,
farther down still, an Egyptian and two more
Turkish batteries—a perfect Gibraltar it was,
this Bulgarian mountain.   The whole army of
the Czarewitch could not have taken it.   "We
shall begin with the artillery," said Baker to me,
"and when you hear the guns open come along
up to the battery on the ridge, and you will have
a fine sight of what's going on."

So back we rode, my henchman and I, through
the deepening shadows of the woods to our
squalid quarters in the village behind the mountain, well assured that, come morning, we should
have something more than a mere skirmish to
chronicle.   An attack in force by the whole army
—the words sounded strange to us, who since
April had been waiting and watching wearily in
camps and towns until we had well-nigh aban-

doned all hope of seeing the Turkish army do anything but cook their rations and cheer the Sultan (several hundred miles away) at the sunset parade. "We will look to the horses," said I to Pomeranian Fritz, "then supper, quick, and turn in." "Yes," said Fritz, "and I have goose for supper, and we finish him for breakfast to-morrow." Tough roast goose is not the best thing, perhaps, for an eve-of-battle supper; and a wild yell from Fritz in the dead of night caused me to think that even a Pomeranian Uhlan's digestion was not equal to it. It was no nightmare, however, but a futile attempt to scare away a dog—one of those strange jackal-like creatures so common in Turkey—which had sneaked into our hut and grabbed the goose. We jumped out of our blankets, and made for the robber, but he vanished into the night amid a volley of boots.— "No goose for breakfast, Fritz."—I was lulled to rest by Pomeranian curses, not loud but deep.

In the morning, between eight and nine o'clock, the sound of the first gun came booming over the mountain, and we were in the saddle and off by

the time the echoes had passed it on. " Ride
steady, master ; I think it will be big fight
to-day." That was faithful Fritz's advice as we
rode off ; he, with his immense sabre clanking,
following close behind. The old soldier's advice,
" Ride steady," was almost immediately found to
be good. We had hardly got to the middle of
the forest when the cannon shots, which had
been quicker and sharper as we neared the battle
ground, became an almost continuous roar, and
Fritz and I suddenly became aware that the edge
of the wood, about half a mile of which we had
yet to pass, was under the fire of the Russian
guns. " Ride steady," again said the Uhlan, as
a big shell came screaming over our heads and
burst against a tree behind us. Another and
another, whistling, tearing, smashing ; ripping off
great branches ; whisking the leaves into the
air ; sometimes striking full against a big trunk
and bursting with terrific roar, the fragments of
iron whirling and humming through the tree
tops, or crashing straight down into the brush-
wood—a hail of leaves, and splinters of wood and

iron, as though legions of devil-monkeys were fighting in the forest. At every crash our horses plunged and reared, now stopping short when a branch came toppling down in front of them; now starting forward with mad bounds when a shell burst in our rear; sometimes wheeling round with a desperate effort to bolt; then, in answer to soothing and coaxing, stepping gingerly along with trembling flanks, pricked-up ears, and staring eyes. It was well for us that we had both been accustomed to the saddle all our lives, and *could* "ride steady." Never before, or since, have I stuck so close to the pig-skin as during that ride through the Kiritchen woods! "The Moscov thinks our reserves in this wood," said Fritz, with a chuckle, "and there be only us!" "And I shall not be sorry when we are out of it, Fritz," said I. "Great noise," said he, "but not much danger."

And indeed we had now passed the dangerous part; the shells went far overhead. We were nearing the edge of the wood, and as the trees opened out we broke into a smart trot, and

P

emerged on the plateau immediately behind our own Krupp battery, which was in action, fiercely replying to the Russian guns. A staff officer came up to me.

"You had better not stay here, sir," said he, in French; "or at least you must dismount and put your horses in a shelter pit."

The whole open space was dug up; shelter-trenches stretched away each side of the battery, and in the rear were holes deep enough, with the parapet heaped in front, to hold the horses of the staff. I had seen something of Turkish skill with the spade, but this was something extra-ordinary; men, horses, guns—all sunk in the ground! Fritz took the horses into the shelter pit, and I ran forward into the battery and looked over the parapet.

A glorious and terrible sight burst at once upon my eyes. From the height, at the very edge of which the battery was planted, an immense extent of country could be seen lying, like a map, beneath. Right and left stretched the ridge on which we stood. Some distance away on the right, in a break of the high ground, were the white houses of the villages of Karahassan and Ketchiler, held by the Russians under Leonoff; beyond them rose the uplands which bound the lower course of the Lom. Immediately beneath us the heights descended in grand wooded slopes to the plain, in which lay the village of Haidarkeui. On our left the ridge continued till it was lost in the spurs of the Derbend Balkan, and in the distance the lovely blue masses of the great Balkans themselves rose against the sky— those mountains beyond which Suleiman the Selfish was frittering away his strength, and denying it to us who were in sore need of it! In the plain to the left lay the villages of Sultan-keui and Ayaslar. Winding through the plain, as far as we could see in either direction, ran the Lom, looking like a pale blue ribbon lying across a carpet of mingled green and yellow and brown. On the other side of the little stream the ground rose in low undulating ridges, on one of which was the main camp of the Russians, over the village of Popkeui. All that country beyond the river was in Russian hands, and it was their advance guard which held Karahassan and Ketchiler on our side of it.

The object of the day's operations became instantly clear to us as we looked out over the parapet of the battery—the Russians were to be driven off the ridge, back over the river. The whole scene of operations lay beneath us like a map, and we could follow every movement of the battle. The landscape alone was worth coming all the way to Bulgaria to see, but now, as we gazed upon it, it was interesting not for river and meadow and mountain, but because it was the field of battle for opposing armies, which would soon be locked in deadly struggle.

"We shall begin with the artillery," Baker had said, and sure enough an artillery duel was now raging, far and wide. Down in the plain behind Haidarkeui a Russian battery of three big guns was pounding away at the wood, and at the Egyptian and Turkish batteries on the lower slope beneath our standpoint. High overhead, on the mountain top, three Krupps were throwing a

plunging fire into the Russian earthwork. Far to
the right, the artillery of Nedjib's division was already engaged with Leonoff's guns at Ketchiler.
For four hours the duel lasted. The Commander-
in-Chief and Staff, and Baker, were up on the
mountain with the three Krupps, watching from
there the progress of the battle. All eyes are
turned upon Karahassan, for that is the central
point of interest. Nedjib's division, descending
from Rasgrad, is to storm the villages and drive
the Russians out. We can hear and see his
guns, and the puffs of smoke draw nearer and
nearer. Nedjib is advancing, and the Russians
as yet are holding on. The single minaret of
Karahassan, standing like a slender white wand
against the dark green background of the slopes
which rise above it, is our landmark, and we turn
our glass on it hour after hour, only looking away
when some keen-sighted artilleryman points to
the Moscov reinforcements, which come pouring
across the plain, marking their track with a little
cloud of dust. Matters are evidently getting
serious with Leonoff.

Meanwhile our three-gun battery continues to
drop its shells into the Russian work at Haidarkeui, and the captain of the guns, stimulated
by the presence of the Commander-in-Chief and
the English officers, does his best.  It must be
a warm place, that earthwork in the plain, for
shell after shell strikes the parapet, and tears
up the ground all about.

" By Jove !" exclaims one of the Englishmen,
"there's a gun dismounted."

All glasses are turned on the Russian battery;
one of the big guns is seen to be knocked out.
Mehemet Ali decorates the artillery captain on
the spot with the Order of the Medjidie, and
the young fellow's face beams with delight.  But
the Russian gunners, undismayed, continue firing
from the two guns, hopelessly overmatched as
they are ; unable to reach the battery which is
raining death and destruction upon them, they
stick to their untenable earthwork, and reply as
best they can.  Gallant fellows !  But their .time
is almost up, for see, now !—an immense column
of smoke rises into the sky from Ketchiler, and

"How Goes the Fight?"

the woods all around are dotted with small quick-darting puffs, which give no sound, but which we know come from rifles. "Ah!" says the Commander with joyful exclamation, "Nedjib is there at last. He has taken Ketchiler." Even as he speaks the base of the rising smoke-column becomes red. It is all over with Ketchiler; the whole village is a mass of flame. Terrible work is going on. The fringes of powder-smoke hang thicker about the hedge-rows, and the field guns on both sides are firing quick, sharp rounds. Leonoff has lost Ketchiler. Can he hold Kara-hassan?—The answer to the eager question unfolds itself beneath our eyes, written on a scroll of fire in letters of blood.

Leonoff is making a gallant stand. Those puffs of smoke which were creeping nearer and nearer to Karahassan are stationary now, and for an hour or more we can see from our height that a pitched battle is raging round the village. "What is he about?" says the Commander-in-Chief, "what can Nedjib be doing? Why does he not bring up his whole division?

Gentlemen (turning to us), the day will belong to him who first brings up his reserves." There, on the plain, we can see the Russian reinforcements hurrying out of their camp at Popkeui, and heading straight for Karahassan, but Nedjib's attack seems to be hanging fire. We only learned afterwards how desperate had been the resistance, how gallantly Leonoff had fought for every inch of ground; how he had looked to the plain, as we to the hills, to see if help was coming.

The excitement grows intense up here in the three-gun battery; we cannot keep still, but must walk nervously about, and even go down the mountain a few steps to get nearer to the fight.

Up jumps Valentine Baker; he can stand it no longer. He asks leave to take a battalion of infantry and attack the Russian right flank.

The Commander says "Yes," and away go Baker and Briscoe and Allix down the hillside and disappear with their battalion into the woods. It will take them a long time to get into action, but that they *will* get there and make themselves felt we know. Baker will waste no time! Another hour; still Karahassan holds out; and now a larger body of Russian troops is seen advancing over the plain. It is the critical moment. The whole length of the ridge where we stand is crowded with soldiers and Bashi-Bazouks, who look out over the battle-field with fierce, eager eyes. We Europeans are the centre of a throng of wild fellows who can see almost as well with their hawk eyes as we with our glasses, but they borrow our binoculars and puzzle over the screw which adjusts them. We explain the working of it, and are amused to see their faces suddenly change as the turn of the screw brings the object into focus. But neither they nor we can make out how the fight is going at Karahassan. If those Russian reserves arrive at the front, Nedjib will not take the village by sundown.

All eyes are bent with eager stare upon the white minaret; our cannon fire has slackened and the two big guns in the Russian work fire

only at long intervals. Suddenly the crowd on
the ridge bursts into shouts and laughter, and a
hundred arms are stretched out :—"See! the
Moscov runs!" A body of Russian cavalry
gallops madly out of the village and down the
slope to the river; presently a dense cloud of
dust is streaming out in the same direction. It
is evident that Leonoff is retreating. He has
lost Karahassan, for, in another moment, what
happened at Ketchiler happens there also—an
immense pillar of black smoke shoots up into
the air, and its base is lurid with the flame of
a vast fire. Almost simultaneously a snow-white
cloud bursts from the edge of the cliff. The
Turkish artillery has pushed through the village
and opens upon the retreating columns. Karahassan is won!

We gaze, fascinated by the magnificent and
terrible spectacle, when our attention is called
off to what is passing immediately beneath us.
"Bizim Askier! Bizim Askier!" is now the
cry—"Our own soldiers!" The plain below
swarms with Turkish soldiers. The Commander,

assured of Nedjib's success, has let loose his
own brigade, and they advance at the double
straight upon Haidarkéui. In a moment they
are over the river, and then spread themselves
out over the fields in open order. The steadfast
Russian battery opens upon them, and we see
the skirmishers lie down. For ten minutes or
so there is no advance; then, suddenly, the
whole brigade rushes at the village, and we see
four mounted officers at its head racing to get
in first.

"We shall have those two guns if they don't
make haste and be off," says Colonel Lenox.

As he speaks we see the gunners limber up
and drive off at a gallop. It was high time!
for the Turkish brigade has gone through the
village and has lapped round the earthwork.
Now all along the heights and from the newly-
won ridge of Karahassan a triumphant salvo
bursts from the Turkish and Egyptian guns;
a deafening cheer rises from the troops around
Mehemet Ali; it is taken up by the battalions
below and spreads along the whole front from

Karahassan to Ayaslar—a joyous defiant shout of "Allah! Allah!" which proclaims the triumph of Crescent over Cross.

\*      \*      \*      \*      \*

And Valentine Baker? He had carried out his flank attack and hastened the Russian defeat. He was reported missing; but I met him on the hillside, riding back to camp, the picture of misery.

"You are not hurt, Colonel, are you?" I asked.

"No—my horse is wounded—but those guns got away! got clear off!—and I could have taken them with a single squadron of English cavalry."

And he rode on without another word.

# CHAPTER XVII.

## Battlefield Horrors.

MEHEMET ALI lost no time in telegraphing to his master on the Bosphorus the details of his victory at Karahassan. It was a jubilant dispatch, of course, but mainly true, whereas the Russian official dispatch was neither one nor the other. "The battalion of Jerusalem redifs," said Mehemet, "captured a cannon, four ammunition waggons, 2,000 rifles, 2,000 coats, and a large quantity of military equipments. The English officer, Baker Pasha, greatly distinguished himself." The Russians said as little as possible, and apparently did as little as possible, until a few days after, when a second terrific blow, delivered at their centre, convinced them that the army of the Czarewitch was in a parlous state, and that they would have to stand

up and fight a pitched battle if they did not wish
to see their line broken through. Meantime the
overwhelming onslaught at Karahassan had
swept them like chaff from the heights of the
Upper Lom. Leonoff's shattered brigades fell
back towards Biela, the Imperial headquarters,
with what haste the spoils of war enumerated by
Mehemet Ali bore witness.

Frank Millet, who was in the thick of the fight
on the Russian side, told the story which Leonoff
dared not tell. " On they came over the open
field, like flies across a plate, firing rapidly with
their guns at their hips. How they fell from the
fire of the Russian infantry at the edge of the
maize field ! We could see bayonets flash and
sabres strike, and we knew they were re-killing
our dead and slaughtering the wounded. On
they came, and before our two big guns were
well placed the bullets began turning up the dust.
As we retired through the walnut grove, the
shells were tearing their way among the trees.
Our wounded were limping back, their white
shirts drenched with blood ; six infantry men

bore a wounded officer, four a hard-hit comrade, four more had a dead officer, stripped naked by the Bashi-Bazouks. All this thinned out the ranks in front, but the soldiers knew too well the fate of the wounded if they were left behind, and they had often enough seen the horrible mutilation of the dead to make them anxious to bring to the rear both dead and wounded. Still the volleys rattled out nearer and nearer, tents were left standing, knapsacks were hastily collected and loaded on the carts which went to the rear, food was left cooking on the fires, the shells came smashing straight into our pleasant quarters. There was a call for matches to set fire to the houses and haystacks and so prevent the nearer approach of the Turkish riflemen. Everybody went back sullenly, leaving camp and baggage. The soldiers, all black with powder, sweaty and dirty, came along by twos and threes, muttering 'Mnogo, Mnogo—there are a great many of them.' "

The day was lost. Millet himself, as he afterwards told me, helped to fire the houses and the

Q

haystacks of Karahassan, and made that magnificent bonfire which was for us who watched the
fight from the Turkish battery on the mountain
top the signal that the day was won!

Of the desperate gallantry with which the
Russians had hung to the villages of Ketchiler
and Karahassan we had ample evidence when
we rode over that part of the battlefield late next
day, but the early morning was devoted to an
inspection of that three-gun battery which had
blazed away at us so steadfastly, and which
Valentine Baker had set his heart on having.
Down we rode, then, into the valley, after a
comfortable night passed upon the stretchers of
the National Society.   The bridge over the river
was broken, but our little Turkish horses
scrambled down the steep banks like cats, and
we were soon in the enemy's country—just now
a sort of Tom Tiddler's ground, where the
chances of being knocked on the head by either
side were about equal.   The irrepressible Bashi-
Bazouk was on the prowl for plunder, and the
Russian rear guard was not far away.   My

companions, who were more cautious than I, and more careful to serve their employers better by not running the risk of capture, declined to ride on to the battery.

"Shall we go, Fritz?" I asked my Uhlan henchman.

"You go, I go," said he, and we went, but only after a careful preliminary stare through our field-glasses.

There, on the crest of the ridge, was the parapet of the battery; close by it rose an ancient tumulus, the summit of which was always occupied by a Cossack vedette. No vedette was there now, but two unmistakable Bashi-Bazouks stood a-top, motionless as statues, looking out over the plain towards the Russian camp. We rode on at once, and, in a moment, were at the deserted battery—three gun-pits, with an extensive parapet, flanked on either side by shelter trenches and rifle-pits for infantry. The ground, inside and out, was ploughed and scored by the Turkish shells, many of which lay about unexploded. How mortal men could have stood

up for ten minutes beneath that rain of shells
was a mystery, but there, as we had seen with
our own eyes, brave fellows *had* stood and
worked their guns all day, their places, as they
fell, being filled up from the reserves. What the
losses were we never knew, for not a single dead
man remained inside the earthwork. There had
evidently been time to remove dead and
wounded from the shameful mutilation which
would have been sure to come in the track of
the Turkish advance.

We were still lingering on the spot which the
Russian artillerymen had made sacred by their
steadfast valour, when suddenly a party of horsemen rode out from behind the tumulus. Russian
cavalry! and we must make a bolt! was the
first thought, with the first glance; but the two
Bashi-Bazouks still stood motionless on the
mound above, and no "Moscov" could be
near.

It was Valentine Baker and his staff, and with
them Colonel Lenox and Captain de Torcy, the
English and French military attachés.

" So *you* are the Bashi-Bazouk we've seen riding about here so long," said the Colonel to me.

" And," added the French Captain, " you are looking for dead bodies, of course."

" There are no corpses to plunder, M. le Capitaine," said I with a laugh.

" There are two over there," he replied, pointing, and we rode up to what looked like a heap of clothes—two fine young fellows in white canvas uniforms ; a few yards further on were their heads. No doubt the scoundrels on the mound knew all about it. Later in the day another party from the camp visited the battery, among them Mr. Ashbury, M.P., who found round the severed neck of one of these heads the little brass medallion which the Russian soldiers are in the habit of wearing. After a kindly caution from Baker not to carry our explorations too far behind the earthwork, he and his party rode on to the camp, and we made for Karahassan through the fields of maize which had been trodden down by the remnants of

Leonoff's retreating force. The ground was littered with all kinds of *débris*, which told of hasty flight, and the condition of the fields would have brought sorrow to the peasants who had hopes of a harvest from them.

Arrived on the low cliffs on which stands Karahassan village, the evidences of the fight lay thickly around—knapsacks, bullets, shreds of clothing. Behind the trees of the wood lay little heaps of empty cartridge cases, showing where a man had stood, firing ; little dark pools here and there told where a man had fallen ; in the gullies by which the cliffs were broken lay many of the unburied dead, stripped naked, their backs riddled with bullet holes. Along the edge of the heights a long line of shallow graves con- tained those who had found hasty burial ; the bodies were scarcely covered. Everywhere—in the woods, in the fields, in the village, even up on the hillside behind it, the horrible stench of a battlefield poisoned the air. In the wood near the village the Turkish infantry was bivouacked, and the horses of a battery of artillery picketed,

the guns being in position at the edge of the
heights overlooking the plain across which
Leonoff's brigades had retreated. Ten times
Leonoff's force could not get back into Karahassan now! From bush to bush, from tree to
tree, from house to house, his brave men had
stubbornly resisted the swarming thousands who
pushed them gradually to the edge of the
heights. So close was the fighting, as a Turkish
artillery officer informed me, that his battery
advanced through the wood, unlimbered, and
came into action again at the edge of the slopes
before the last of the retreating Russians had
got beyond the foot of them.

"There lie some of them, you see," said he,
pointing to the white bodies down below.

"Yes," said I, "but how is it that they are
stripped naked, these poor fellows?"

"We have nothing to do with that," said he,
with a proper French shrug, "the irregulars are
responsible for that."

"But the dead men's heads are still on their
shoulders," I remarked.

"Ah!" he replied, "Monsieur has observed some of our curious Eastern customs."

And then, with a pleasant smile, he asked me to go and have some coffee *à la Turque* in his tent.

After bidding good-bye to the artillery captain we went on to Karahassan, and all that we had seen faded into nothing before the terrible spectacle which burst upon us.

More than half the village was on fire, and the flames were roaring and crackling on all sides—houses, barns, stables, fences, all were involved in a common destruction. The roadway was littered with ashes; thousands of printed leaves, torn from Bulgarian Bibles and religious books of the detested creed, lay scattered about. Bashi-Bazouks were pillaging and ransacking the houses which the flames had not yet reached; burial parties were at work digging shallow graves, or heaping the earth over the bodies as they lay; wolfish dogs sneaked about, ravenous but terrified; overhead the carrion birds wheeled around, kept from alighting by the roaring flames and the ascending smoke. The trees were torn and shattered by the shell-fire.

A Turkish cemetery at the edge of a wood had been stoutly defended by the Russians, who used the tomb-stones as shelter. The advancing artillery had shelled them out of the graveyard, and the quaint fez-topped tomb-stones were split and chipped.

It must have been a warm place, that cemetery, the living fighting above the dead, and the air filled with hissing fragments of shattered iron and splintered stone. Many a new grave was added to the number that day.

We could find no quarters in blazing, reeking Karahassan, so we rode on to Ketchiler, a mile or so farther on. Here there remained some half-dozen houses only. The village presented an extraordinary appearance from a distance. The ground on which it once stood was covered with square patches having grey borders and black interiors; the squares were the foundations of the houses, covered with charred beams, the grey borders were the remains of the enclosing fences. The ground-plan only of the once smiling little hamlet remained! The trees, which, as in all Turkish villages, grew among the houses, were scorched and burnt by the flames. No living thing was there except dogs and owls.

Wearied with our long ride, and sickened by sights and smells, we dismounted at a wretched hovel, and took possession of it for the time. Melton Prior, of the *Illustrated London News*, joined me, and we set about getting a rough-and-ready meal before rolling ourselves up in our blankets for the night. And when night fell the loneliness of the place became terrible. There was a little yard at the back of the house, and we went out into it to forage for some wood for our fire. As we stepped out of the back door we met a sight which made us start with horror. There in the dim light lay a gleaming white naked body, prone, arms stretched out, fingers bent, and without a head. It was the climax of the horrors of the day; but we were too weary to shift our quarters, and we slept well enough, never even dreaming of the terrible thing which lay so near us. We gave it decent burial in the morning.

# CHAPTER XVIII.

## Hearing the Czar.

I T takes no great knowledge of strategy or of
tactics to be quite certain that, when you
have given your enemy a hard knock, which has
made him "see stars," it is advisable to give
him another by way of preventing him from
coming up to time.

Mehemet Ali had given the Czarewitch's
advanced brigade a "facer" at Karahassan, and
every one thought that on the very next day
the whole of his army would advance all along
the line of the Lom, and smash in the Russian
centre. But poor Mehemet could not get *his*
centre to move. Nedjib's division, which had
struck so hard and so well, was flushed with
victory, and fit to do anything. Valentine Baker
and his staff of fire-eating Englishmen were busy

night and day feeling ahead, and they reported
that the Russians could not stand against a
general advance. Off went the Commander to
hurry on his centre, and he left orders that Prince
Hassan and the Egyptian troops were to push
on beyond Karahassan and harass the retiring
brigades which had been defeated there, while
the greater portion of the victorious division
which had defeated them was moved along to
reinforce the sluggish centre and help it to strike.
Baker and his officers were to act as Hassan's
pioneers. Five whole days elapsed before the
centre was able to fight, and meanwhile the
Egyptian contingent, so far from harassing the
discomfited foe, simply went on cooking and
eating their dinners in camp.

Baker and his staff pushed across the river up
to the ridge over Popkeui, on which had been
the Russian camp. He saw beneath him in the
valley beyond the whole of the Russian infantry
in full retreat, with a long baggage train and
fourteen guns. Two field guns with a regiment
of infantry could have captured the whole of the

baggage train and the fourteen guns. But when this magnificent opportunity was brought to the notice of the Egyptian Prince in camp—as it was, of course, in hot haste—he would only send cavalry, unsupported; and when Baker, making the best of it, took a few squadrons, the Russian infantry turned at bay, and would have simply eaten the Egyptian troopers, horses and all, had they ventured to attack.

Baker could do nothing. The fourteen guns got clear off, to his unutterable disgust. What he, and Mehemet Ali, when he heard of this *coup manqué*, said to the Prince is not known; probably policy and etiquette prevented their language from being forcible or free, but they no doubt thought what all of us who were not tongue-tied made no scruple to say—that if all the black-faced mob with guns, which called itself the "Egyptian Contingent," were marched to the rear, back to Varna, and re-shipped to Alexandria, the loss to the Turkish Empire would not be great, even at a moment when every man, who was a man, was wanted.

What Egyptian troops can do when officered by Englishmen we now know, but in 1877 the fighting capacities of the fellaheen were not discovered, or discoverable. Later on, when at last Mehemet Ali had got his army to move, the Egyptians again failed him ; but this lost opportunity proved to Baker at least that there was no depending on them. Fourteen of the enemy's guns to be snapped up, and no one ready or willing to snap—that was what sank like iron into the soul of our dashing ex-colonel of hussars !

On the fifth day after Karahassan the Turkish centre struck out, and once more the Russian line was crumpled up by the terrific onslaught of the Ottoman infantry. They plunged into the fight with all the confidence which the now well-proved superiority of their weapons had given them. For they had found out that the clumsy Kranka rifle of the "Moscov" was no match for the Martini-Henry, and that while the Russian fighting distance was 400 yards they could come into action with deadly effect at twice that distance.

The battle at Kaceljevo was another severe defeat for the Czarewitch; the second week of September saw the Russian line in full retreat upon their next line, the Valley of the Black Lom. There they would have to stand; if they could not hold that line they would lose their bridge, and the next battle would be decisive as to their continued existence in Bulgaria. Such were the Turkish anticipations. Vain hope! Within a fortnight this victorious Turkish army, which had swept down like a tornado and scattered the infidel like chaff, was slinking back to the fortresses, baffled and broken, never again to reappear as an army in the field. The failure of Mehemet Ali's advance meant to the Sultan the loss of Bulgaria; Suleiman, the traitor, and his supporters in the Palace, were responsible for that failure.

After the second blow at the Czarewitch had been successfully delivered at Kaceljevo there was nothing to prevent the advance of the Turkish army, and it advanced in the leisurely fashion characteristic of all Oriental movements.

There was no pushing out of bodies of cavalry to worry the Russian rear-guard, no galloping horse artillery, no cloud of skirmishers pressing the retreat; the advance took place in a solid mass; the whole army slowly moved in as the Russians moved out. And so, a week after the two battles, we found ourselves ten miles nearer the Russian Imperial headquarters. At Popkeui, which was within sight of the battle field of Karahassan, we were within twenty-eight miles of the Czar, and there was ample evidence of the importance of the place to the Russians, for on the high ground above the village were the extensive gun pits and shelter trenches which had been thrown up to defend it. The blow at Kaceljevo had made the position completely untenable. All round were graves of the Russian dead who had been borne to the rear from the field of Karahassan—saved from insult and mutilation, but buried so hastily that the bodies had become uncovered. Many were already dried into mummies by the heat of the sun. Here and there upon the ghastly forms

R

were shreds and patches of what had once been
the uniform of their corps. The Russian graves
at Popkeui were among the most terrible of the
horrors of the campaign.

The village itself had escaped serious injury;
and those peasants who were bold enough to
return found their homes much as they left
them; doors and shutters had gone to light
camp fires, but walls and roofs remained. In the
deserted Bulgar house which I annexed for my
quarters were two immense wine casks, the
heads of which had been knocked in. A Turk,
who stood at the door watching my culinary
operations with great interest, grinned with
delight as he told me that the Bulgar owner
had fled and abandoned the brimming casks
to the Cossacks, to his own Giaour friends!
The Bulgarian school had been completely
gutted by the Bashi-Bazouks; the pictures were
slashed, books were torn and scattered about.
Everything that told of education or religion
was the special aversion of the Bashi-Bazouk.
To dig his knife or bayonet into the face of a

sacred picture, to tear the leaves of a book into a thousand pieces, gave him almost as keen a pleasure as to cut the throat of a wounded man.

As the Turkish army rolled heavily along on the direct road to Biela, the Russian line fell back before it. The Czarewitch's outposts, which in August extended from the Danube, right away south to the Balkan, along the White Lom, had now dwindled and shrunk. A process of concentration went on as the Turks advanced, and this, we knew, would result in another battle more severe than Karahassan or Kaceljevo. But where would the Russian stand take place? Upon which of the ridges, rising in successive waves like Atlantic rollers between us and the Czar, would Turk and Moscov meet again? That was the question. Baker was the man who could first find the answer, but he had no cavalry to speak of, and the reconnaissance work of the army was of a primitive description. Time and again Baker and his officers were the scouts of the Turkish army. Our gallant ex-cavalry officer, and the few young Britishers who formed

at once his staff and his escort, were ever in the
front, far beyond the army, often close to the
Russians, so close that sometimes they had to
ride for their lives.

What a haul that would have been for the
Moscov! With what a shout of joy would the
announcement of the "Capture of the Englishman, Baker," have been received at Biela, at
Plevna, at St. Petersburg! But Valentine Baker
was hard to catch. Wide awake as weasels,
slippery as eels, he and his Englishmen were
gone before the Russian dragoon could unsling
his carbine, or the Cossack couch his lance. The
Turk likes to reconnoitre, as he likes to do everything, at his ease. With great ingenuity he
erected charming little leaf-thatched bowers as
look-out stations. In them, sheltered from the
sun, he would sit for days, looking steadily to his
front, and his keen eyes would instantly detect a
Cossack lance as it rose over the next ridge.
But to scour the country far and wide, to ride up
hill and down dale in quest of the enemy, to
advance cautiously, to retire precipitately, all this

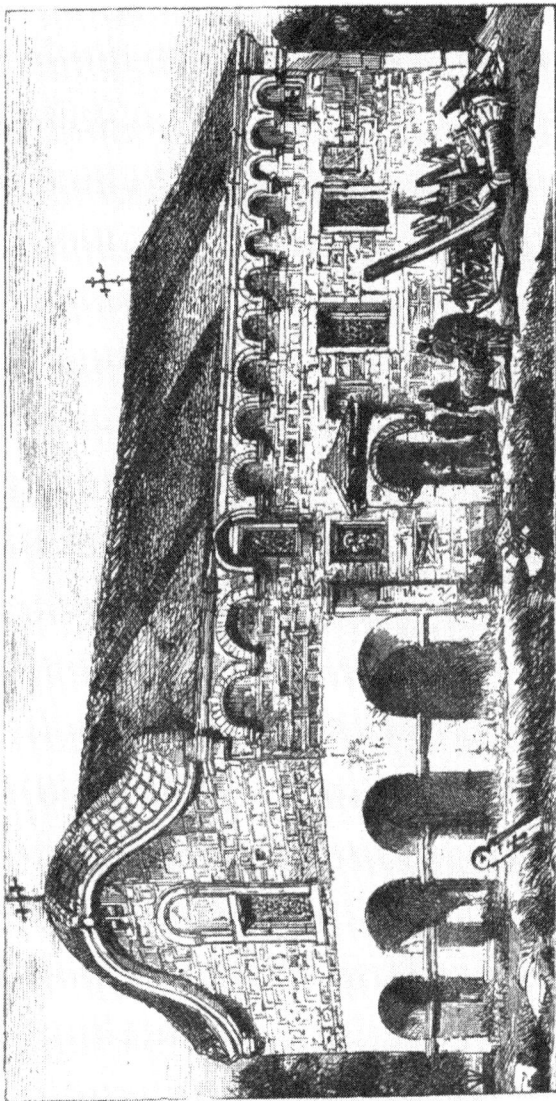

BULGARIAN CHURCH AT KOPATCHÉ.

(From a Drawing by the Author.)

he regarded as unnecessary excitement, which neither hastened nor retarded the destined battle. The irregular Circassians, Bashi-Bazouks, and other miscellaneous scoundrels, were the scouts of the army, and did fairly well, but they were always for their own hand—it was loot first and duty last with them.

Next to Popkeui came the occupation of Kopatchè, still nearer the Russian headquarters. Its charming little Bulgarian church was instantly sacked and plundered, and the churchyard was littered with scores of icons, or sacred pictures, everyone of them with the slash of a sabre or the dig of a bayonet in the face of the personage represented. I spent a long time in examining the pictures. Many seemed to be ancient and valuable examples of the Byzantine school of painting. The yard glowed with gold and colour, when I had turned the pictures and their fragments right side up. Saints, madonnas, crucifixions, emblems, inscriptions in Greek— the entire decorations of the church had been stripped down and flung out of doors, and here they lay for anyone to pick up who cared for them. Works of art are not desirable as a portion of the baggage of a war correspondent, but when I came upon "St. George and the Dragon" I felt as though I had come across a bit of old England in that far land, and I walked off with my patron saint. The painting went through the campaign with me in my saddle-bags, wrapped in a flannel shirt, and it hangs on my wall facing me as I write now.

# CHAPTER XIX.

## In the Victor's Track.

IF it had been possible for us war-correspondents simply to accompany the Turkish army in its advance after the Russians were driven back from the line of the White Lom, we should have been saved from the necessity of detailing many of the horrors of the campaign. All wars are horrid; but in the case of those between civilised peoples the horrors are, so to speak, conventional. Hardship and disease, wounds and death—these are seen in a hundred forms, and after a while they cease to impress soldiers and civilians with their terror; the feelings become hardened by the constant sight of sufferings which are part and parcel of the whole business. "We are in for it and must make the best of it; flinching means failure"—

that is the guiding maxim for soldiers and civilians alike in war time, and the observance of it accounts equally for bravery in battle and patience in hospital. When men have brought themselves to that frame of mind, minor hardships go for nothing. A night in the rain on the bare ground, the loss of a dinner, a pint of water to wash in, no chance of a clean shirt for a fortnight—these things are borne with a more or less genuine grin. But the Russo-Turkish war of 1877 was quite an exceptional campaign, and those who were engaged in it, as combatants or onlookers, were daily confronted with exceptional occurrences. It became immediately apparent to all the witnesses of the battles in which the Turks were victorious, that *no wounded Russians were ever brought into Turkish hospitals.* Swarms of Bashi-Bazouks and armed camp-followers overran the battlefields immediately after the close of the engagement, and with our own eyes we saw them mercilessly butcher the helpless wretches who had fallen. I have already spoken of the massacre of the wounded

Russians who had crawled beneath the trees for shelter at the preliminary skirmishing for the Kiritchen heights, and of the horrors that accompanied the Turkish assault on Leonoff's positions at Ketchiler and Karahassan. As I have said, if we could have gone on with the army, without retracing our steps, we should have escaped the knowledge of many more atrocities almost too dreadful to tell. The full tale of the horrors of 1877 has never been told; the deeds of the "Legion of Vengeance" on the one side, and of Bashi-Bazouks and Circassians on the other, would form a chapter of horrors unique in the history of modern warfare. I cannot write such a chapter, but I believe that in this book of mine many of the terrible events of 1877 are made known for the first time.

It so happened that while we were waiting at Kopatchè for Mehemet Ali's next move forward, the arrangements made by the " Political Commission" for the "assistance," as they called it, of the special correspondents, broke down. While the army lay in the fortresses, the Political

Commission was in fine feather, and lorded it
over us poor "specials" without check or
hindrance. But when campaigning in the open
began, and it was a case of every man for
himself, and the devil take the hindmost, the
Commission simply evaporated; it melted into
air, thin air; it left not a wrack behind. The
war-correspondents, therefore, simply "chucked"
the Commission, and, after its first astonishment
that such a thing could be, the Commission felt
quite relieved to think that it *could* quietly dis-
solve without anyone being a penny the worse.
When a correspondent had a letter to post, or a
telegram to send, he would despatch a mounted
messenger with it twenty or thirty miles to the
rear, or, if advisable, take it himself. Being a
light weight, and as hard as nails, I did much of
my own letter-posting, and in my rides over the
battlefields which marked the victorious track of
the Turkish army, I was brought face to face
with those horrors, which, as I said, made this
war unique. I made no attempt to hunt out
atrocities, but simply noted down at the time the

facts which came under my observation, and the narratives of trustworthy eye-witnesses.

It was, of course, in the ruined villages of Karahassan and Ketchiler that the most terrible things occurred; in passing through them on the way to Rasgrad, many days after the battle, evidence met us at every turn that the struggle had been, beyond measure, ferocious and blood-thirsty. Two or three days after the battle I rode back from Kopatchè through Karahassan to post a letter fifteen miles farther on. As I was tightening my horse's girths for my long ride, one of the English doctors strolled up to me. "Are you going back through Karahassan?" he asked; "if so, mind your horse doesn't stumble over any of the heads; they are lying about as thick as peas." But I saw no heads in the road, and thought my medical friend had been having his little joke at my expense. When I came to the spring and the stone trough wherein my companions and I used to wash, when we lived in the village, I saw that the doctor had made no joke. There, in the ditch into which the trough

drained, was a heap of heads! A myriad flies
rose in a cloud when I approached, and I looked
down upon the grey face that lay uppermost—a
young man's head, with crisp, light hair, the
swollen eyelids tightly closed, the mouth half
open. Beside the heap lay some kepis bearing
the number "140." Such was one of the
trophies of Karahassan, a truly Oriental trophy
—a pyramid of the heads of the vanquished—
and so it was regarded by one of the villagers
who had joined me, and who took no pains to
conceal his triumph in the presence of my pity.

"These poor Giaours' heads seem to please
you, my friend," said I.

"They are the heads of my enemies."

"But I suppose when they were fighting and
lost their lives you went away and hid."

"I was here, in Karahassan, and I saw the
Giaour turned out."

This is a man to be interviewed, thought I,
and so, cultivating his farther acquaintance by
means of a liberal baksheesh, and warning him
that something awful would happen to him if

he told me any lies, I noted down one or two incidents which I extract from a stained and battered note book.

During the assault on Karahassan, Nedjib Pasha, who commanded the main attack, was standing beneath a tree (carefully pointed out to me by the villager), watching the progress of the fight. The victorious battalions were raging through the streets, maddened by the desperate defence, when suddenly one of the soldiers rushed out of the ranks, holding aloft the head of a Russian impaled upon his bayonet. "God is great, Pasha!" he shouted, making straight for the colonel, "behold the head of an infidel!" Then, lowering his rifle, he drew the head off against his foot, and left it there on the ground in front of his commander as a war offering. Nedjib, who was a humane and enlightened man, turned away with an angry exclamation of disgust, whereupon the soldier, nowise abashed, promptly ran his bayonet through the head again, again brandished it on high, and, with a fierce cry of "Allah! Allah!"

went on like a madman down the blazing street. "And you saw this?" said I to the villager.

"I saw it," replied he, with the air of one who had had a real treat.

A little farther on, the Nizams (regular troops) had taken a Russian officer prisoner, and had relieved him of his revolver, sword, and watch, but offered him no violence. Soon afterwards a battalion of Redifs (reserve) came along, and the unfortunate man was instantly butchered.

Another and more fearful story was vouched for by doctors of the Stafford House Society. By the side of the main road, which was the line of advance of the attacking brigade, lay the naked corpse of a Russian soldier, with a stake driven into his body. As the advancing troops passed this shameful spectacle they broke into brutal jests and laughter. Years after, in the Soudan, I remembered this incident, reminded of it by a curious discovery on the battle-field of Tofrek.

Throughout the Mohammedan world the same strange customs and crimes prevail; the hideous scenes I had seen perpetrated in Bulgaria by the Turks I saw repeated, in the self-same manner, by the Mahdist tribesmen around Suakin. The Turkish officers to whom I spoke about these things deplored them, but at the same time recognised in them a more or less just retribution for the deeds which they said the " Legion of Vengeance " had perpetrated south of the Balkans — the women whose henna-stained fingers were hacked from their hands, the fifteen other women who were locked into a house, abandoned for a while to the lust of the Bulgarians, and then burned alive.

Thus it was that, for nigh upon three weeks after the victories of Mehemet Ali on the Upper Lom, we were obliged to ride back and forth over the ground which had been so desperately fought over, and to see and hear of the terrible incidents which had accompanied the Turkish advance. There was no escaping from the horrors and atrocities; our path to the rear, between the army and the fortresses,

S

lay through a reeking charnel-house; we had
to pass through the valley of the shadow of death
in those terrible pilgrimages. If we could only
have passed it blindfold and holding our noses!
To emerge from it, on our way back to the
front, and to find ourselves in the sweet, restful
quarters we had annexed at the village of
Kopatché, was for my companion of the
*Standard* and myself the best reward for the
most unpleasant duty we ever had to fulfil.
Four miles beyond us lay the main body of
Mehemet Ali's army; we were well clear of
them; ten miles behind were the loathsome
battlefields—we were well clear of *them*.

The little wrecked church, with its graveyard strewn with sacred pictures, was to us,
for a few happy days, a pleasant and peaceful
abiding-place. There we lived in two hovels
which we annexed, and we made ourselves
quite at home in somebody else's property.
The village was full of wheat, rye, and
barley, stacked by the vanished inhabitants
in their gardens, abandoned by them to the

Russians and by the Russians to us. Millet
and his box of matches had not been there,
and so our overworked horses had plenty of
grain. We slept on beds of unthreshed wheat,
our servants built us a "gourbie" of branches,
cunningly arched and tied together, and covered
with masses of splendid barley—a sun-proof,
weather - proof bower of delight. With the
rye we lit our fires and bedded down our horses.
Our possession of all this luxury was not un-
contested, for a day or two after we had
squatted, a Turk presented himself at our
door and announced himself as a "villager"
of Kopatchè, and the owner of all and singular
the tenements, goods, and chattels of which
we had made seizin. He carried in his girdle
a remarkable variety of edged tools of no
possible use in husbandry.

"These are my houses," said he, "and I
want to live in them."

"But *we* are living in them."

"They are mine."

"You are a Turk; is it not so?"

" It is so."

" Then how did you come by a house in the Bulgarian quarter of Kopatchè? Did you live among the Giaours ? "

Our villager· became very thoughtful at this question, and, after a prolonged stare, which we returned with stony eyes, he abandoned the attempt to blackmail the rich " Ingleez Pashas."

# CHAPTER XX.

## The Eve of the Decisive Battle.

OUR two fighting pachas, Valentine Baker and Salich, the Englishman and the Turk —the eyes, ears, and brains of the advancing army—were busy in those days of September. They, and their small reconnoitring force of English officers and Turkish cavalry, hung upon the rear of the Czarewitch's retreating battalions, followed them step by step along the main road towards Biela, where lay the Czar, occupying each ridge as the Cossack rear-guard left; and, though never fighting, yet pressing the retreat in a manner which must have been extremely inconvenient to the Russians. It could not go on for ever; the gradual retirement of the beaten troops of Leonoff meant also gradual concentration; it soon became evident that, as soon as

they had fallen back far enough to be in touch
with the main army of the Czarewitch, the latter
would send out a force large enough to arrest the
retreat, and then, choosing a position covering
the road, he would make a stand and dispute
Mehemet Ali's advance. Where would that
position be, and when would the fight come off?
Those were the questions of the minute, the
hour, and the day. The energetic reconnaissances
of Baker and Salich soon enabled us to make a
fair guess at the answer, and when the next move
of the headquarters was made to a village called
Voditscha, four miles farther on and within a
day's march of the Imperial camp, we knew the
decisive moment was rapidly approaching.

My companion of the *Standard* was already
packing and loading up when I drove back to
our hovel at Kopatchè one evening with the
latest news from headquarters. A friendly Bashi-
Bazouk had told him of the orders to advance ;
we both set to work, and within an hour we were
carrying out our own little strategic movement to
the front. At Voditscha we went through the

familiar process of annexing an empty house—
not a difficult process, seeing that the village
was, like all the others along the route traversed
by the retreating army, empty and desolate.
The whole Bulgar population—men, women, and
children—had gone over to the enemy, the men,
no doubt, doing good service for their liberators
as drivers of waggons, hewers of wood, and
drawers of water.   To deal with the women and
children was probably a more difficult and delicate
matter.   They had disappeared from the villages,
and found an asylum, such as it was, within the
belt of country held by the Russian armies.
Their places were promptly filled by the stream
of Turkish villagers which flowed in the wake of
the Ottoman army.   If their own homes in the
reoccupied villages were destroyed, the returning
Turks annexed the Bulgarian quarter, and thus it
happened that, during our advance, the candidates
for the possession of the Bulgarian houses were
of all nationalities—English, French, German,
Italian, Turk, and I know not what others ;
only the Bulgar himself had no claim to his

own. Poor Bulgar! he was bandied about like a shuttlecock between Russian and Turkish battledores.

Here, then, at Voditscha was probably the last halting-place before the decisive battle. From the entrenched camps at Rasgrad and Eski Djuma, the Turkish field army had descended upon the Czarewitch's line, swept it away in spite of the gallant stand at Karahassan, and was now almost within striking distance of the Czar himself. One more successful blow, and gallant Osman at Plevna would be relieved. Throughout the advance we were much struck with the wonderful aptitude shown by the Turks in maintaining their telegraphic connections, and in making roads for the passage of their troops and artillery. Wherever Mehemet Ali went, he had a telegraph instrument under his fingers, and kept up direct communication with Constantinople. The wire was raised on poles or stretched from tree to tree along the whole line of advance. The telegraph is one of the few Western institutions, *à la Franca* as they call them, which the Turks are able to

appreciate. Their language lends itself singularly
to telegraphy, and the generals and pachas of the
army delighted to sit at the end of the wire, and
chat for hours with their friends at the other end
in the intervals between coffee and cigarettes.

Another matter of surprise to us was the
remarkable skill with which the Turks used the
spade. The typical Ottoman, we had been led to
believe, cannot dig, though he is nowise ashamed
to beg ; he was, as we thought, a warrior, pure
and simple, who disdained implements of husbandry.    But it is certain that in road-making
and in throwing up earthworks the Turk is hardly
to be beaten by any Western people.    I have
mentioned how in a marvellously short space of
time roads were cut through the thick woods up
the difficult heights of the Kiritchen ridge, and
how Krupp field-pieces were dragged up to the
very summit of the Sakar mountain, which
dominated the battle-field of Karahassan.    The
roads were solidly constructed, practicable for
heavier guns than 9-pounders, and batteries were
thus established at points which at first sight

appeared quite inaccessible to artillery. No sooner was the road cut and laid to the required spot, than gun pits were sunk, shelter trenches dug, and powerful redoubts thrown up in a twinkling. In the course of a single night the edge of a ridge on the top of a hill, which was before an unbroken forest or a smooth field, bristled with Krupp guns, and suddenly became an almost impregnable stronghold. In the use of the field telegraph, and the construction of military roads and earthworks, the Turks in 1877 were on a level with the most advanced Powers of Europe, and their proficiency in those important matters was brought out by the war, to an extent which appalled the Russians and surprised all Europe.

Hardly had we settled down amidst the fleas and offal of Voditscha, when, on the 20th September, a reconnaissance by Baker and Salich resulted in the discovery that the Russian retreat had stopped, that a powerful army had concentrated, and that the Czarewitch stood at bay. Correspondents were not expected to approach

the positions of the army immediately before a
battle, though during the battle itself they were
cordially welcomed where the shells fell thickest
and the bullets hummed loudest.   A correspondent or two less was a matter which the
Turkish headquarters staff regarded with great
complacency, but the presence of the ubiquitous
journalist in a freshly-made earthwork acted upon
them like a red rag on a bull.   They went for us
on sight.   We, for our part, had to take the bull
by the horns, and when the news of the Russian
" Halt, front!" reached me, I determined to
make a reconnaissance on my own account, and,
if possible, get a glimpse of the enemy's position.

Looking carefully to the horses and riding
gear, I started with my Uhlan on this rather risky
enterprise.   A mile of road brought us to a one-
gun battery at the end of the ridge, and, to our
surprise, the Russian position lay right before us.
It had not been far to seek!   The major in
command of the shining little Krupp fraternised
with me, and pointed out the position of the
Moscov and of the Turkish batteries.   There,

on a bare rounded ridge which seemed to extend across the valley, lay the enemy; his camp fires were plainly visible, and we caught, now and then, the flash of a bayonet, and the gleam of the polished metal of field guns in position on the crest. It was evident that the Russians were in force upon and behind that hill, and would dispute with us there the possession of the road.

"So the Moscov will stand there and fight us," said I to the friendly major.

"He will," said the major, "and perhaps to-morrow *we* shall stand there."

He made an ineffectual attempt to dissuade me from riding down into the valley to the outposts. "The Moscov is there, and many Bashi-Bazouks," he said. "It is better not to go, but if you must go, ride very slow." I can see now his kindly smile and courteous gesture as he bade me farewell.

Poor major! before the sun set on that morrow he lay in his shallow grave, under the green turf close to his little one-gun battery.

The path led down through dense thickets of

brushwood, and was guarded at intervals by cavalry pickets. The troopers were lying in the shade with their horses tethered, and two men were detached as outposts from each picket. My magic pass cleared the way for us, and at last we reached what we supposed was the advanced post; the two sentries seemed to be more vigilant than the others, for they were perched high up in the branches of the trees, the barrels of their Winchester carbines poking out threateningly from the leaves. But beyond these we came upon a band of Bashi-Bazouks, seated in a circle in the wood, discussing the probabilities of imminent stratagems and spoils. A highly picturesque sight the scoundrels made—a bright ring of colour and flashing weapons in the leafy wood. We reined up to look at them. They were around us in an instant. Having established our influence—partly by our absolute indifference to what was at first a rather alarming situation, and partly by means of the gold-sealed paper, we demanded all the news they had to give.

"Yes, Effendi," said the leader, "there are

many Moscovs just in front. Cherkovna (the village beneath the Russian position) is empty. A Bulgar came down from the ridge where the Moscov lies and entered the village. We saw him, and (with a grin which displayed a remarkable set of teeth) he did not go back."

Under the circumstances we abandoned our intention of going into Cherkovna, which was evidently a sort of Tom Tiddler's ground, and after bestowing a baksheesh upon the brigands, we rode back past the vedettes and the two fellows in the trees, receiving from them in passing a peculiar smile, which seemed to have a touch of irony in it. In another moment we came plump upon a whole regiment of Turkish infantry, which was being reviewed by a Pacha and his staff. They were riding down the line away from us, but we recognised at once that it was Salich himself, the man of all others to whom special correspondents were as gall and wormwood. Beside him we thought we made out the form of his Serene Highness Hassan of Egypt, who from the height of his serenity condescended also to disapprove of journalists. We took to the woods. Had I been haled up before Salich, and had he ascertained that I had been up to the advanced posts, nothing would have saved me from arrest, my pass notwithstanding; so, as I did not wish to miss the coming battle, I gave the Pacha and the Prince a wide berth, and circumvented the regiment of infantry.

Thus it was that on the eve of the battle I obtained a fairly complete idea of the positions of both armies. I had got as close as possible to the low, rounded hill which had been chosen by the Russians as their defensive position—a bare slope, cut into terraces, and sparsely dotted with trees. I had seen that their works consisted of gun pits and shelter trenches; that the whole hillside was dug over with rifle pits ; that the position was of great strength. On the Turkish side I saw that batteries had been established on the highest points opposite the enemy, and that they dominated the Russian position, though at very long range. The preparations for a decisive battle were complete. The Turks, flushed with

victory, and encouraged by their unopposed
advance thus far, were eager to strike another
blow. The Russians had clearly made up their
minds that Mehemet Ali should advance no
farther.

As we rode slowly back in the afternoon, a
dense fog came down and shut the opposing
armies from each other's sight. A solemn stillness, broken only by an occasional trumpet-call,
reigned in the camp and upon the hills around it ;
the long line of watch-fires, which lit up their
summits and marked the position of the Turkish
lines, was shrouded from view. We groped our
way through the silent streets of the village,
and lay down in our clothes upon the straw
for a few hours' sleep, with a strong presenti-
ment that if the fog lifted at daybreak we
should hear the sound of the guns, and know
that Mehemet Ali and the Czarewitch were
trying conclusions.

" It will be hard knocks to-morrow, sir," says
Fritz, after we have rolled ourselves up—" get
plenty sleep."

And a pleasant sleep it was, if only in my
dream a sweet English village, with great trees
and grey church tower, had not got mixed up
somehow with a bare, brown slope, gashed with
trenches, and bristling with cannon!

# CHAPTER XXI.

## Defeat.

THE 21st September—eventful day for the destinies of Bulgaria — broke dull and gloomy upon the two ridges, where lay the hosts of the Czarewitch and Mehemet Ali. The fog still hung over the country; just such a fog as shrouded the heights above Sebastopol on that November morning when the Russians delivered their attack at Inkerman. Perhaps in the Russian army, now within two miles of us, there were some veterans who had served there, and they, too, may have recalled that Crimean battle morning. "Hallo!" said my colleague, as he got up and looked out into the fog at daybreak, "here's a regular Inkerman morning. I wonder whether they will attack us instead of our attacking them." There were no signs of any such intention. On the part of our own commander there was no disposition to take advantage of the fog.

Valentine Baker and his merry men were, as usual, first in the saddle. It was understood that during the night a large force of artillery and infantry was to be moved up to the chosen position, overlooking Cherkovna village, and fronting the ridge which the Russians had fortified.

Baker was there by daybreak, but he found that the position had not been occupied in force, and that, though the earthworks were ready, the guns were not in them. Our energetic ex-colonel of Hussars sent one of his English aides galloping back to headquarters with a message stating the fact. The Pacha's reply was to the effect that it was not quite certain whether the mist was going to rise or not—after which, no doubt, he turned round and had forty winks. Had the Russians felt disposed for Inkerman tactics, and advanced in force under cover of the fog, they might have ensconced themselves comfortably in *our* empty batteries ; but it was clear that they had no idea of forcing the fighting.

By eight o'clock the fog had disappeared, and the Turkish troops commenced to move about in all directions, in full sight of the enemy. Across the valley we could see the Russians, now fully alive to our intentions, getting up their heavy guns, manning the trenches, and strengthening their position with finishing touches on either flank.

A council of war had been held in the evening, under the presidency of the Commander-in-Chief. Baker, Salich, Prince Hassan were present, and the plan of attack had been decided. The first proposal was a feint on the Russian right and a direct attack in front. This was not carried out. Another plan was substituted. The feint was to be a serious attack ; a whole division, composed of Egyptian and Turkish troops, was to be hurled at the Russian right, and some other attack was to be made, when or where nobody seemed to know. The division which was to attack the enemy's right was to be allowed two hours to develop its advance, and then our centre was to complete the Russian discomfiture. Excellent plan, if only the enemy would allow himself to be discomfited!

Our eighteen guns were in position on the ridge by the time the sun had struggled through the mist and dispersed it; ten in the centre, three on the right, five on the left, six in motion— twenty-four Krupps in all, with plenty of ammunition, and admirably manned. Opposite them, at an average distance of a mile, were twenty Russian guns, heavier than ours, and quite as well served; so that the artillery balance was against us.

At nine, the flanking division started on its enterprise; by eleven our glasses disclosed their skirmishers issuing from the wood, ready to commence the attack. Almost at the exact time appointed, the crack of a Krupp in our central battery, and a white ring of smoke skirring away into the air from its muzzle, showed that the battle had begun. Instantly the whole ridge burst into smoke and flame ; in another moment a long white cloud seemed to leap out of the brow of the ridge on the other side of the valley ; yet another instant, and, as the roar of the Russian guns reached us, the ground all round was torn and scored by bursting shells.   Clouds of dust rose suddenly from the face of our batteries, as the enemy's shot struck full on the parapets. Over yonder we could see similar clouds shooting up from the Russian earthworks.   Both sides had the range, and every shot told.   So excellent was the enemy's practice that the Commander-in-Chief gave strict orders no one was to go to the edge of the ridge, and no one was to remain mounted. We put our horses into shelter trenches and sat ourselves down on the parapet to watch the artillery duel.

It was worth taking the risk to see such a sight, and we remained awhile watching the shells as they burst all around the Turkish works, hopping up over the ridge, and tearing the ground at each ricochet.   Now one of the big guns would send a shell smack against the face

of our central battery, and as the thundering roar
burst forth, a great dun-coloured cloud would rise
high in the air, pierced and riven with the flame
and smoke of the replying Krupps; then another
shell would come screaming over the battery
and plunge into the wood behind, ripping and
cracking the tree trunks; a third would just
graze the edge of the slope, ricochet into the air,
and drop into the battalion massed in the hollow
behind. Then there would be a sudden stir, a
little crowd would gather, and in a few minutes
the laden stretchers would be going to the rear
with the poor stricken wretches whose bodies and
limbs had been shattered. And they seemed to
hop into the air so gently and to be so easy to
avoid—those big shells! We soon found out
that one of the most uncomfortable of the mixed
sensations which accompany the consciousness
of being fired at by heavy artillery, is the impossibility of discovering which way the shells
are going. When they seem to be coming
straight for you they burst a hundred yards
away to your right or left; when they seem to be

well on your flank—plump! they are at your feet, and you have barely time to fall flat on your stomach before the devil's own din is rattling about your ears.

Even the excitement of watching an artillery duel, and dodging shells, palls after a while, and after two hours of it, we got our horses out of the pits and rode off to a spur of the ridge on our right. From there we had a complete view of the whole battle-field. The bare hill, held by the Russians, lay immediately before us, and we could see their gunners blazing away from six earthworks. It was long past the time when Ismail's Turco-Egyptian attack on the enemy's right ought to have been developed, but we had not looked long before it became evident that the head of his column had come in contact with the enemy. We could see faint lines, and jets of smoke streaking and dotting the ground. A fierce infantry fight was raging, but why was Ismail two hours late? Two whole precious hours after the appointed time!

Now we see a movement in the hollow behind

our central battery, a sort of compression of the two great black masses of troops which had remained so long patient under the ricochet fire. "Our centre is about to attack," exclaims one of our military friends of Baker's staff. As he speaks, the notes of the bugle reach us, and we gallop back to our first position to witness the advance. The two columns are in motion; they advance up out of the hollow in two dense masses; they reach the summit of the slope; the bugles sound again; instantly the masses break up and spread out on either side upon the crest of the ridge; once more the trumpets ring out sharp and clear, and the whole line—with a fierce shout of "Allah!"—disappears over the brow.

It is not in human nature to resist the terrible excitement of the moment. One and all, regardless of orders, we ride forward to the edge of the hill, and watch the brave fellows go down. The whole line descends into the valley, the field officers, dismounted, leading their horses down the slope. A tremendous roar bursts out from the Russian ridge; a salvo of artillery greets the advancing Turks; the side of the slope is shattered and torn by bursting shells, and we see scores of gallant men rolling down, dead or mortally wounded.

Now the battalions have reached the bottom. One of them makes straight for a triangular grove of trees on the slope of the Russian hill, beneath the centre of the position. The possession of the wood is fiercely contested, but soon we see the Russian skirmishers falling back, and presently the edges of the wood are fringed with white smoke. The Turks have carried and occupied the grove. Two Russian horse artillery guns gallop forward, unlimber, and begin shelling the wood; but the brave battalion clings to it. " No support from our guns. By Jove, it's hard on that battalion!" says one of the English aides.

We leave the crest of the ridge and return to the headquarters staff, which is anxiously watching the development of Ismail's attack. Things are going badly. Ismail was not only late, but instead of throwing the whole weight of his fifteen battalions upon the Russian flank, he sent

only three battalions into action, and carefully
kept the others out of fire. The three battalions
behaved with the greatest courage—they were
Turks—but the others, Egyptians, it appears,
would not face the music,

" Gentlemen," said Mehemet Ali, turning to
us with his usual affable smile, " the situation
is critical."

Prince Hassan of Egypt, who wore a huge
pair of yellow boots, and looked like a first tenor
at the opera, contemplated his toes in silence.

Salich, Baker, Taborvitch (the hero of the ride
from Vienna to Paris), Colonel Lennox, and
many other officers who were in the group,
seemed pre-occupied.

What was to be done ? The afternoon was
closing in, and no impression had yet been made
upon the Russian position. All hope of using
the Egyptians was abandoned ; but down in the
valley, under the Russian hill, the Turkish
battalions were clinging to the slope, and maintaining an ineffectual fire upon the earthworks
above them.

Finally, Mehemet Ali resolves to send down another battalion to their support; the scene we had already witnessed is enacted again, and in still more stirring fashion. The battalion advances by fours, at their head their colonel, with his sword in one hand and a stick in the other. Why a stick? *They* do not want driving into action, these gallant fellows! Their uniforms are weather-stained and ragged, but their step is light and springy as they go swinging along to the crest of the hill. As they spread out into line of companies their war cry bursts forth—"Allah! Allah!" It is answered by a thundering crash, which announces that the keen-eyed Russian gunners have seen them. Down they go, through the ruined village and up the slope. And now a terrific infantry fire is directed upon them from the centre of the Russian hill;—evidently the Czarewitch's reinforcements have arrived!

But not a man of those brave battalions falters or turns back. To advance up to the earthworks is clearly impossible for them, but

in two steadfast fighting lines they hold their
ground.

It is six o'clock now, and the cannonade dies
away on both sides; but when night fell those
Turkish battalions were still on the hill-side.
We could see the flash of their rifles on the now
dark background, making a belt of fire along the
slope. An *aide-de-camp* is sent to fetch them
back.

"We are all right here," was the message
the officer in command sent back, "and can hold
on all night."

A more peremptory summons was sent, and
at last they come reluctantly back.

"I have never seen such splendid and devoted
bravery," said Baker, "anything could be done
with such troops—if those who handle them only
knew how to do it." What *he* did with them,
afterwards, at Tashkessen, on the other side of
the mountains, is well known.

Such was the battle of Cherkovna, or, as
Mehemet Ali requested us to call it, "an
offensive reconnaissance of the Czarewitch's

position." Had Mehemet Ali driven the Russians from the ridge it would have been a "great victory," but, under the circumstances, it was only an "offensive reconnaissance."

The simple truth is that the battle of Cherkovna was a most serious defeat. That it was not a disastrous rout was due to the weakness of the Russian force, and to the undaunted valour of the Turkish private soldier.

The last hope of relieving Plevna was gone. Osman was lost!

THE ROAD TO CONSTANTINOPLE.

# CHAPTER XXII.

## 🕮etreat.

BEATEN! After weeks of careful pre-
paration—so careful that not a gaiter-
button was wanting; after a victorious advance
which had swept the Czarewitch's troops from
their advanced positions as if they had been so
much chaff, driven in their line, and sent it
reeling back twenty miles. Beaten!

When those gallant battalions which had clung
to the hillside had yielded to the repeated
orders of the commander and had come back,
the sputtering fire died away; night fell on the
disastrous battle-field of Cherkovna; there was
nothing to mark the presence of man on the
great slope, save the Russian camp fires which
flared along its summit. The dead and wounded
lay there thickly, and there, until the sun rose

next morning, they remained, shut out from sight
of friend or foe by the dark night, which brought
cool breezes to comfort the dying, and shrouded
in kindly mantle those who had no more need of
man's help, or Nature's.

This, then, was the result of the offensive
campaign of the Army of the Lom, begun with
so much care and—up to the time when this
fortified hillside confronted them—conducted so
gloriously by the Ottoman soldiery.

Poor Mehemet Ali! Useless now for him to
reiterate his complaints of Suleiman and of the
insubordination of his own generals. He had
made his attempt and failed; failure meant
instant dismissal. From the commander to the
camp-follower, all knew the penalty of failure for
a leader of Ottoman armies. In the old days it
was the bowstring at Stamboul; now it is
banishment to Arabia, where, after a little while,
a cup of coffee, most politely offered, answers the
same purpose.

We rode back to our quarters that night with
the uncomfortable conviction that, unless the

general intended to make another attack in the morning, the Russian army would be "prospecting" in our direction before breakfast time. To ascertain what was our plan of campaign for the morrow was an impossibility. Things get very much mixed in the camp of a beaten army, and the question was not whether we should go up to headquarters and ask what was going to be done, but whether there were any headquarters at all. After riding about in the dark, stumbling upon pickets (very dangerous), running plump against limbered-up batteries of artillery, bumping into baggage mules, and generally incurring the risk of being fired upon as " Russian cavalry in pursuit," we gave it up and crawled back to our den at Voditscha. There, after meagre bite and sup, we lay down in our clothes, dead beat, and in a moment we were in dreamland.

It seemed to us as though we had only been dozing a few minutes when the faithful Fritz burst into our room and roused us with a shout—
"Up, sirs, quick! The Turks are gone, the Russians are coming." "Turks gone, Fritz;

what the devil "——— We rush to the door of the house; it is broad daylight; not a living thing is to be seen; the village is deserted; not a single tent remains on the ridge above it.

"Pop on the saddles quick, Fritz." In a twinkling girths are buckled and bridles slipped on.

"Look now," says the old Uhlan, pointing suddenly to the entrance of the village, "Cossacks!" Sure enough, over the brush-wood, just beyond the houses, is a clump of spears. Not a moment to be lost! we must mount and off, or we shall be prisoners. Our baggage mule is abandoned; an excellent shoulder of mutton is abandoned; my watch and money are somewhere in the straw; my companion's boots cannot be found. "Quick, or they catch," was Fritz's cry. We swing into our saddles and ride off at a gallop up the silent street. Three miles without drawing rein, and then we take a look back. No one in sight! We have got clear and our Cossack friends are making merry with our belongings. For money and clothes we don't mind so much, because we had little money and few clothes; but the shoulder of mutton! And we have nothing but a couple of biscuits and a small flask of whiskey between the four of us—sorry breakfast for four hungry men. But we consoled ourselves with the reflection that things might have been worse —if the whiskey had been left behind, for instance! It was not a meal to linger over, and we had to keep sharp watch as we ate. Capture by Russian cavalry meant for us a sudden termination to our career in Bulgaria. As Englishmen on the Turkish side we should not have been honoured guests in the Russian army; the Cossacks would probably have soundly kicked and cuffed us, after they had plundered us of the little we had left, and then we should have been conducted to the rear and interned, perhaps interred, at Bucharest.

On we pushed, after this brief halt; mile after mile in the scorching sun; past deserted houses, rotting crops, abandoned fields. Now and then we came upon a cluster of new-made graves, some of them scratched open by prowling dogs. Our path was strewn with the litter of armies. Four times had the tide of war rolled over this unhappy district in alternate advance and retreat. As the Russ advanced the Turkish villager fled; as the Turk advanced the Bulgar disappeared; and now, as we rode back in the rear of the beaten army, neither Turk nor Bulgar was to be seen. The harvest was dropping from the ear, for there was none to gather it. We were in a complete solitude, more dreary, more mournful, than the solitude of the African desert. An abandoned house is a sadder thing than the Sahara.

There is not much chance to philosophise when one is between the rear guard of a beaten army and the advance guard of its pursuers; but such thoughts did come into our mind in fragmentary fashion.

But where *was* the Turkish army? We had now ridden ten miles pretty fast, and had seen nor man, nor horse, nor gun. Of all rapid military manœuvres we had ever seen or heard of, that night retreat of the entire Turco-Egyptian army was the most astonishing. "It's the quickest scootle ever I saw," said my companion. Fritz, the Uhlan, merely remarked scornfully, "They go back quicker than they came." But where? We were in the broad track of their retreat (there was but one way back to the shelter of the fortresses); the ruins around us and the half-buried corpses told us that plainly enough.

There was nothing for it but to ride on. We longed for a half-hour's rest under the shade of a tree, or on the floor of one of the shattered houses. We longed, with an exceeding great and bitter longing, for just one cut off that shoulder of mutton. As we stopped beside a spring to drink, and water our horses, a happy thought struck Fritz. He was shampooing his horse's nose and legs; then he suddenly mounted.

"You wait here ten minutes, sirs; I will ride on very fast and find dinner."

Dinner! why the man must be mad.

"All right, Fritz, good luck to you;" and off
he went at a gallop.

The ten minutes passed and no Fritz re-
appeared, and we rode on for a mile or so.
Our spirits sank, so did our horses' heads, and
we soon subsided into a walk. We were passing
along a plain dotted here and there with oaks.
Suddenly a little cloud of smoke puffs out
from behind one of the trees; we hear the
swish of a bullet, and see the dust fly up just
ahead of us. Ping! swish! once more; and
rather nearer this time. My companion's
servant gallops up and joins us. "From that
tree, sirs; it is a Bashi-Bazouk." A third
shot sings past us. Missed again, but, hang
it! we can't go on being fired at like this.

Out revolvers and gallop straight for him—
that's the only thing. We dashed at the tree,
and before the B. B. could fire again we were
upon him. He glared at us as we shouted,
"Yok atesh" — "do not fire," and it dawned
upon him at last that we were not Moscovs.

"Why have you fired at us?"

" I thought you were Moscov horsemen."

" Do you know at whom you have been firing? Look here!" and I presented to him the Imperial seal. Poor Bashi collapsed; his knees smote together; his eyes sought the ground. Had we proceeded to hang him to the tree he would have quietly accepted his fate. He surrendered his rifle and yataghan.

"Very well," we said, "you made a mistake; we pardon you. Take back your arms, but find us some dinner."

His eyes brightened as he handled his weapons again—warlike ruffian that he was!

" Allah be praised, Effendi, it is well; come with me."

Fritz now came into sight, cantering heavily towards us. " See Fritz," we said, "we have made a prisoner, and he will take us to dinner." " I found no dinner, sir," said he, "but I have found the rear guard." " How far is the army from here," we asked the Bashi. He pointed in the direction from which Fritz had come and said, " Half an hour, there."

"It is well," we said, "lead on, O Bashi-Bazouk."

Within a mile there stood a Bulgar farm-house. We rode up to the yard and shouted. Presently, much to our surprise, a man came out.

"We want food; bring out for us what you have."

"What I have, Effendi! I have nothing."

"We *must* have food."

"The army has been here; I have nothing; I am ruined."

The Bashi-Bazouk here stepped forward. "Quick, dog! or you will be shot," he shouted, glaring fiercely at the Bulgar, who grew positively livid with terror at the sight of his deadly enemy. He went into an outhouse, and presently emerged, leading a small and lean ram. In a twinkling Fritz and the Bashi had tied its legs, and it was laid across the withers of the Uhlan's horse. Mutton for dinner after all!

"Take this money for your ram," we said, giving the Bulgar a gold piece, which my companion produced. "No," replied the poor cringeing creature, "no, sirs, never mind that "— and he shot a quick, terrified glance at the Bashi-Bazouk. "Take it," we said, "and if this man comes back and robs you, we will have him hanged for firing at us ; remember." The Bashi, baulked of his prey, followed us out of the yard, after having bestowed upon the Bulgar several epithets in choice Turkish.

And now for the rear guard ! Half-an-hour's gallop and we came plump on a battery of artillery unlimbered and ready for action. There is a stir among the guns as we come in sight. We take out our handkerchiefs and hold them up. An officer rides out. We salute.

"Do you know where you are, gentlemen ? Are you aware that you are between the rear guard of the Turkish army and the Russian cavalry ? " '

" We are very well aware of it ; we have been in that position since daybreak."

The officer laughs. "You have been fortunate, messieurs. You have successfully evaded the Cossacks, but in another moment my battery would have blown you to pieces. As it is, I must place you under arrest."

"No need for that, captain," we said, and out came the magic document.

"Ah! that is all right. I am delighted. And you have a sheep? Come to my tent and rest. Soon we shall dine. My battery remains here for the night, and the whole army is just beyond."

\*      \*      \*      \*      \*

That quiet, cool tent under the trees! The coffee and cigarettes which just took the sharp edge off our appetite! The siesta! The dinner! strips of ram rolled up and roasted—"kebab" of ram!

Captain of artillery, may your shadow never grow less! for it was to us as the shadow of a great rock in a weary land.

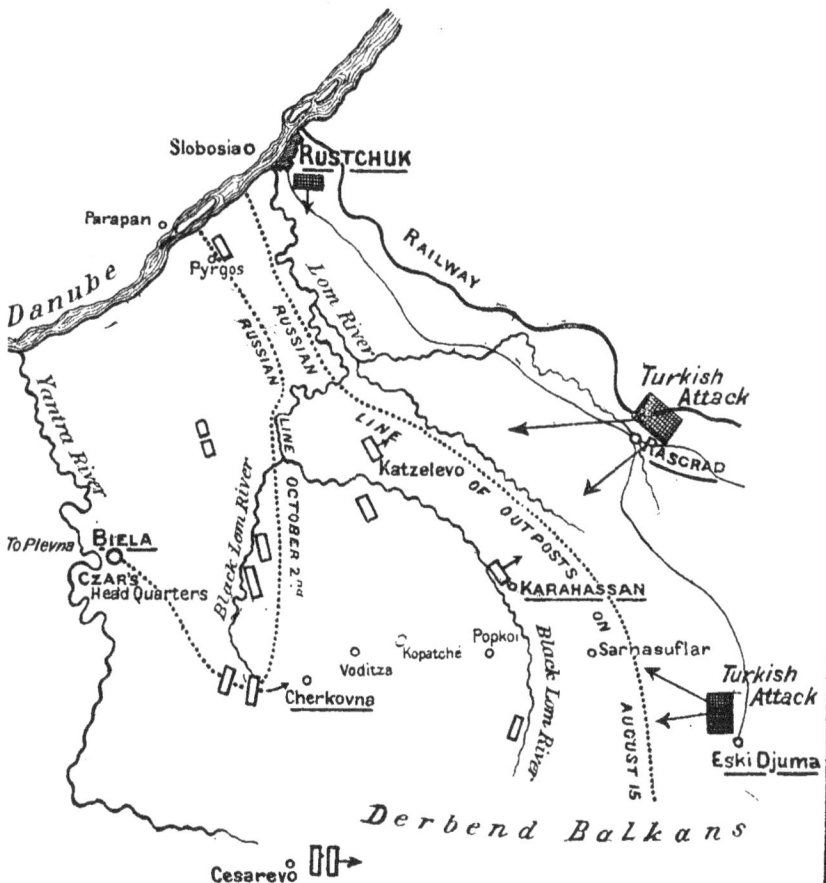

Map to illustrate
MEHEMET ALI'S ATTACK
on the
ARMY OF THE CZAREWITCH.

Turks..... ▮
Russians. ▭

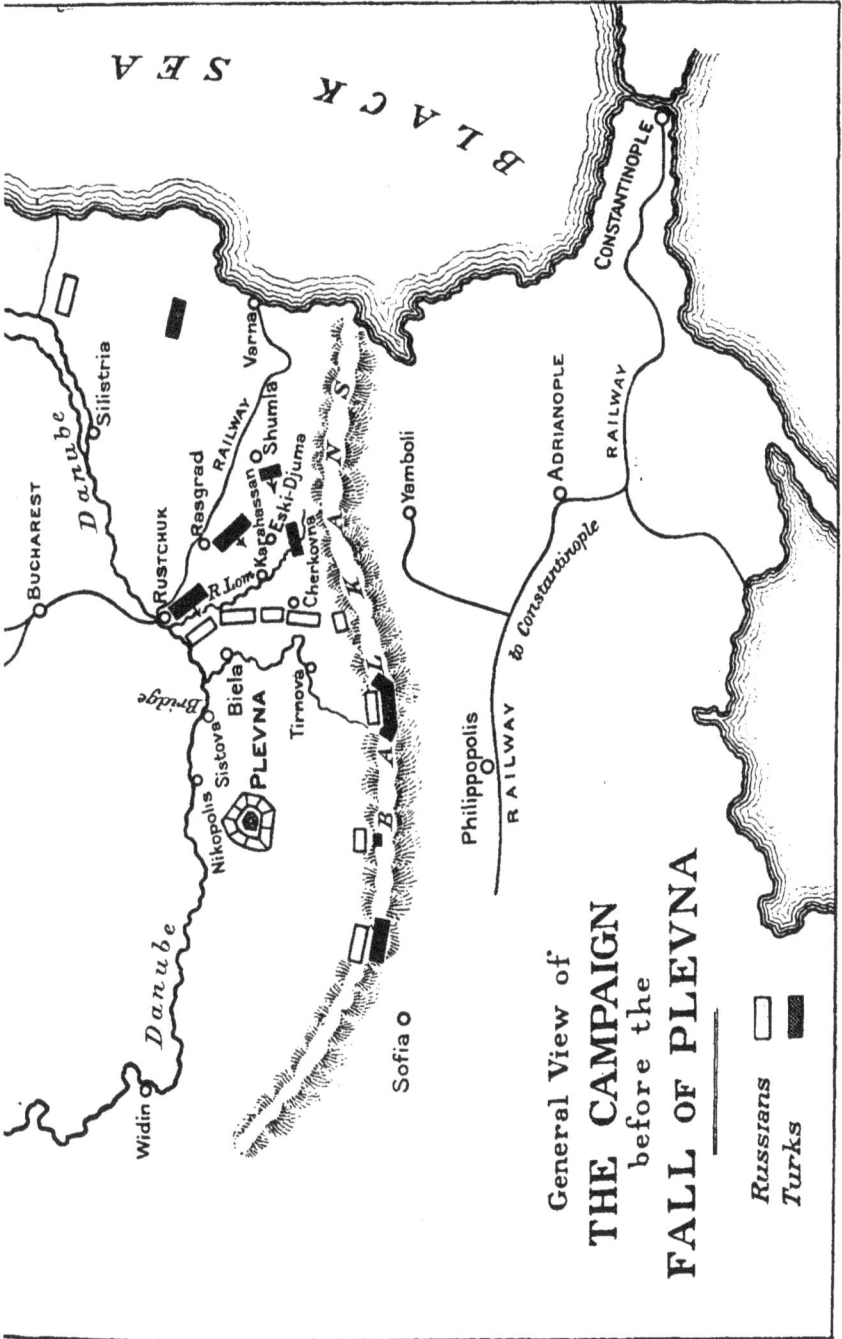

BLACK SEA

Silistria

Danube

Bucharest

Varna

RAILWAY

Resgrad

Shumla

Karahassan
Eski-Djuma

RUSTCHUK

R. Lom

Cherkovna

Yamboli

BALKANS

Bridge

Biela

Tirnova

PLEVNA

Sistova

Nikopolis

Philippopolis

RAILWAY

Sofia

Danube

Widin

ADRIANOPLE

RAILWAY

to Constantinople

CONSTANTINOPLE

General View of
**THE CAMPAIGN**
before the
**FALL OF PLEVNA**

*Russians*
*Turks*

www.ingramcontent.com/pod-product-compliance
Lightning Source LLC
Chambersburg PA
CBHW020808100426
42814CB00014B/377/J